BACKPACKER How to Travel the World

Carl T. Fransen

PACKERBACK Press

Calgary/Canada

Although the author has tried to make the information as accurate as possible, he accepts no responsibility for any loss, injury or inconvenience sustained by anyone using this book.

BACKPACKER: How to Travel the World

Library and Archives Canada Cataloguing in Publication

Fransen, Carl T., 1973-
Backpacker : how to travel the world / Carl T. Fransen.

ISBN 0-9738475-0-6

1. Backpacking--Guidebooks. 2. Travel--Guidebooks.
I. Title.

GV199.6.F72 2005 796.51 C2005-903881-0

Packerback Press

http://www.aworldtraveller.com

First printing: June 2005

Printed in Canada

You don't know if you are going to love it or hate it until you do it.

- Carl T. Fransen

Table of Contents

Preface

December 11, I was sitting in the Madrid Barajas International Airport with my faithful backpack sitting on the floor between my legs. I was nearing the end of my backpacking trip and was going to catch my flight home to Canada. This would be my last city I would visit after travelling the world. I had been to over 37 countries and visited over 200 cities throughout North America, South East Asia, Western Europe, Eastern Europe, Scandinavia, The Baltic Region, and Africa. I reflected and asked myself, "What now?"

Fifteen months prior, I started as a novice packer excited to be entering my first country, South Korea. I was hoping that all of my preparation and research had been enough and I was ready for my backpacking tour around the world. I spent a couple of months prior trying to make sure that I had adequately packed everything I needed, had enough money, got enough vaccinations, etc.

Unfortunately, while I was backpacking I realized that there were some things that I had forgotten to bring and that I had packed things which I didn't need. I also had to learn the ropes as I travelled. Even the basic tasks such as finding a safe place to sleep, where to eat good food, what to do in a new city, when was the best time to leave, how to communicate, etc. were skills that I had to learn as I went along.

Overtime, I got the hang of it. I began to really like travelling. I enjoyed all the opportunities and experiences it gave me. I can easily say that I matured more in that time travelling than I have at any other time in my life.

Backpacking to me was a life investment. It is something that I hope everyone has the opportunity to experience. I want to inspire you to travel. I want to show you how easy it is to take the first step and the next until you are travelling the world. To make a guide that will get you out of your comfort zone and to try something new and potentially very rewarding. I decided to write this book to help you do just that.

Everything that I have learned during my travels is written down here. It will answer a lot of the unknowns about being a backpacker and travelling the world. This book is your companion for planning, travelling and eventually coming home from backpacking.

Considerable effort went into creating a guide that would not go out of date or become obsolete over time. Many travel guides are only good for a short time after they are published. Countries change, cities change, and what was once an amazing destination could become a place to be avoided. The basics on how to successfully backpack are mostly universal. Also, the information and experiences that are presented here can be applied to nearly any country you are planning on visiting. The goal of this book is to give you enough knowledge to encourage you to backpack and explore the world.

The book is divided into four sections: Introduction, Getting started, On the road, and Coming home.

The Introduction is an overview of who and what a backpacker is and what backpacking is all about. When someone backpacks around the world, what is it like? What do backpackers do? It is a good idea to see if backpacking is a type of travel you might be interested in before you start.

The second section, Getting started, is a complete guide of what to do before you start travelling. It details all the preparations that will help with a safe and successful travelling experience.

The third section, On the road, is what you need to know while you are travelling. You are going to face daily challenges such as how to find a place to stay, where to eat, how to get help, how to cross a border, etc.

The fourth section, Coming home, is about readjusting to life when you come home. After such an experience you may encounter reverse-culture shock and I will give you some suggestions on how to 'fit in' again.

Note: Everything contained within this book is based on my personal experiences and a very small amount of research once I arrived home. I tried to provide the best advice I could. Please understand that this book cannot guarantee that you will have a positive experience while backpacking. My goal is to give you the boost you need to help with a lot of the unknowns when first starting out. I encourage you to find your own style of backpacking that will work for you. And remember, that this book is like a smorgasbord, take what you want and leave the rest.

Happy travelling!

Carl T. Fransen
Adventurer, World Traveller, and Generally Nice Guy
Backpacked to over 150 cities and 30 countries

What's a backpacker

Introduction

Thousands of people from all over the world choose backpacking to be their preferred way of travelling. Is backpacking right for you? Would it be something you are interested in? What is the difference between a tourist, backpacking in the outback, and backpacking around the world? This section will help answer all these questions and gives you an idea on what backpacking around the world is all about.

What is backpacking?

Backpacking is an economical way of travelling anywhere in the world. Backpackers go to the same places as tourists but tend to stay in cheaper accommodations, eat at less expensive establishments, and take lower class transportation. Everyone has a backpack that contains all of their possessions for the duration of their trip. The goal is to save your money, but still travel to wherever you like, and do whatever you find interesting at in any given location.

Some people mistakenly say that they are "taking a year off" or "taking a break from school or work" to go travelling. Backpacking is not taking time off or taking a break from life, it is actually another type of education that can be both challenging and rewarding. Travelling the world places you in many different situations and you begin to learn more about yourself and life around you. It's the kind of education you cannot learn by reading a book (even this one) or going to any school. It is "experiential learning" that will give you more rewards than you ever believed possible.

I would stress that backpacking should not be considered a holiday or a vacation. A holiday or a vacation is more for taking a small time out from your regular life, going someplace exotic to relax, unwind, and recharge. After that short period of time is over you come home, feeling better, and go back into your old life. Backpacking is where you don't mind roughing it a little bit and skimp on a few creature comforts. You face more day-to-day challenges since you are choosing to stay in less "touristy" areas. By doing this, you are able to discover and immerse yourself within new cultures and ideas, and removing yourself from the "tourist bubble". Backpacking provides daily challenges and teaches you to use your abilities to adapt and survive in new environments. I found that backpacking is more of a life investment than a holiday.

Why backpack?

There are many reasons why backpacking is beneficial. You become more self-reliant and confident. The more you travel, the more backpackers you meet and friends you make around the world. You have the freedom to come and go as you like and your next destination is completely your choice.

You learn to adapt to different environments. Each time you step off that bus you realize that you are not going to be able to speak the local language, you don't know where you are going to sleep for the night and you have to figure out where there's a good place to eat. This is your daily adventure: you are responsible for finding a place to sleep for the night, where and what to eat, what you are going to do once you are there, and where your next destination will be. You are in charge of how much or how little fun and adventure you are going to have.

Each destination offers new challenges and activities that you can choose to do. I go out of my way to place myself into these situations just to experience something new. These are opportunities that you could never have had back home. All you have to do is take the opportunity.

If you are interested in some of my adventures in backpacking around the world, check out my other book, *Backpacker: The Journey Begins*. I wrote about the good, the bad and the ugly, complete with pictures.

Here are some of what I did while travelling:

- Climbed three active volcanoes in Sicily. One was still exploding and the other two had sulphur and steam vents continually going off.
- Became a certified scuba diver. I was in the third best diving spot in Thailand in water that was 27 C with the most amazing fish and coral I have ever seen.
- Learned how to speak Spanish and improved my French. I finally had a chance to put my other language skills in use.
- Met awesome people, travellers and locals that have changed and influenced my life. I took away a lot of great memories from the people that crossed my path.
- Attended operas in Austria, and musicals in England and Spain. All I did was walk up to the ticket booth, buy a ticket, and enjoy.
- Walked through the world's best art galleries and museums. Back at home, I would have to read a book or go on the Internet to see the Mona Lisa.
- Taught martial arts to Buddhist monks in Laos. I was at a mountain temple where I taught a group of novice monks Aikido.
- Meditated for ten days in silence in Thailand. This was gruelling and by far, one of the most intensive activities I have ever done.
- Partied in Spain with 30,000 other people. Carnival! Party all night and sleep all day.
- Went climbing in the Alps.

- Met my relatives in Sweden. I was the first in my generation to go back to the motherland and find my relatives.

While travelling, you can make friends with not only friendly locals, but other backpackers like yourself. Your fellow backpackers come from their own unique culture but you already have something in common with them. You are both away from home and looking to try something new and possibly exciting. It is common to hook up with a group for a little while and explore your new surroundings. Before you part ways, you exchange e-mail addresses and potentially you have a place to stay if you ever visit their country. The locals often want to show you the best of their country and will go out of their way to show you around. They will take you around to all the little known places that tourists haven't discovered yet.

Backpacking also allows you go where you want, stay as long as you want, and do what you want on very little money. Even on a budget you are able to do many exciting things. Best of all, you tend to go to the less "touristy" parts and be exposed to what life and culture is really like.

After travelling to a few places, you get a better understanding of how the rest of the world works. You have to interact with the local people on a daily basis on such basic things as transportation, food, accommodation, etc. Often, you will find that your preconceived notions of what a place is like are incorrect. Those notions will be challenged and the result will be a deeper and broader understanding based on first hand experience, not stereotypes.

A Backpacker – a summary

The following are some generalizations on who and what a backpacker is. This should help you get a basic understanding of what a backpacker lifestyle is all about.

Age Group: The youngest backpacker I met was a 17-year-old girl from Chile and the oldest people were a married couple from the United States who were 73 and 74 years of age. On average, most backpackers were between 18 and 30.

Duration of the trip: A regular trip for a backpacker would last anywhere between 2 to 3 weeks to 2 to 3 years. I met a Japanese girl in England who had been backpacking for over 7 years. She loved the freedom. When she was low on money she took a job or two in whatever place she happened to be in at that time. Then she would keep on travelling.

Luggage: All backpackers have one thing is common, they all carry backpacks (most with detachable day packs). A backpack is a mobile, durable, light weight, travel bag that can be taken nearly everywhere. It allows you to have both hands free at all times and straps securely and comfortably to your body. Since your backpack is not dragging on the ground like a suitcase, you can cover nearly any type of terrain from stairs, streets, gravel roads, trails, etc.

What to bring: Backpackers only pack the essentials, foregoing many luxury items for the sake of limited space and weight. It is smart to carry the least amount of equipment with you for the widest range of environments.

Adjusting: It takes a week or two to get used to the backpacking life style. At first you are a little unsure on where to sleep, how to move, what to eat, etc. Afterwards you get more comfortable, you can experience the freedom that backpacking can offer.

Accommodation: A backpacker will usually look for the cheapest accommodation in the local area. We choose to stay in hostels, "pensiones", guesthouses, campgrounds and one-star hotels instead of somewhere more expensive. Simplicity is best. All that is required is a secure place to shower and sleep. Also, feel free to find some accommodation in a five star hotel.

Community: Backpackers stick together and form a support network for each other. In every hostel, it is easy to find friends to hang out with for the duration of your stay. This happens automatically since everyone has things in common – they are all travellers, are new to the city, are often alone, looking for something to do, and are in a place with other like-minded people.

Food: Backpackers usually avoid restaurants as a first choice because they tend to be more expensive. The best place is to get food is at the local grocery store or marketplace. Street vendors are also a good idea.

Transportation: A backpacker will use nearly any inexpensive form of transportation to get from point A to B. No-frills discount transportation is the way to go. Night buses or trains, affectionately called the "red eye express", can save you time and hotel expenses because you can sleep on the way and wake up at your destination.

Costs: As inexpensive as possible. Roughly, what a tourist would spend in two to three weeks is the equivalent of what a backpacker would spend in two to three months.

Freedom: You go wherever you can get a visa or a border stamp. You can stay as long as the country allows and when you get bored of one place, you can pack your bag and head to your next destination.

Why: Backpackers want to see the world, experience new cultures, and learn and do it all economically and with a good deal of personal freedom and independence.

Summary

Being a backpacker is safe and easy. It is up to you on how much luxury you want to have. One day you may decide to camp in a near by campground and the next you may splurge on a five star hotel. It is up to you on what you are going to do. One day you are a couple kilometres inside a cave and the next you are attending a classical opera. Each backpacker is different and has their own styles of travelling styles.

Getting started

Introduction

I had to learn how to travel as I went along. Without any previous experience or seasoned backpackers to talk to, I found myself guessing a lot. Prior to leaving, I had searched for backpacking books in stores, the library, and the Internet and didn't find any concise "how to" guides, even on how to get started.

Before you arrive in your first country, there are some things that you should take care of. Doing the work beforehand will potentially save you from some problems and make your journey safer and more enjoyable.

The following is a detailed plan on nearly everything you need to do before you start your journey. Doing the work ahead of time will help ensure a more successful trip.

The checklist

When I first made my checklist, I had a grand total of ten items. I was hoping that I had covered everything but still, I had no real idea of whether I had. If I were just beginning to travel for the first time, the following would be my checklist. Every item in the checklist is covered in much greater detail in the following sections.

- ❑ Apply for and secure a valid passport or make sure your current passport will not expire while you're travelling.
- ❑ Get an idea of which countries you want to visit and how long you are going to be travelling.
- ❑ Buy a guidebook that covers all the countries you are going to visit.
- ❑ Consult a travel nurse and get necessary vaccines for your chosen countries. Most medical clinics and

doctor's offices can give you the contact information for the travel nurse in your area.

- ❑ Purchase the needed medicines and pills recommended by the travel nurse. Be sure to follow the directions carefully.
- ❑ Put together a definitive first aid kit.
- ❑ Purchase all necessary gear.
- ❑ Place money in two bank accounts (one primary and one backup).
- ❑ Buy emergency travellers' cheques.
- ❑ Do some preliminary research on your areas of interest.
- ❑ Notify friends and family your plans.
- ❑ Check with your country's foreign affairs office to obtain information on the entrance requirements, visas, length of stay, issues, etc. In Canada, this office is called DFAIT (Department of Foreign Affairs and International Trade), but the name will change depending on which country you live in.
- ❑ Open an Internet e-mail/blog/etc. account to stay in touch with everyone.
- ❑ Consider giving a parent or trusted person power of attorney over one of your bank accounts.
- ❑ Buy travel insurance for the entire duration of your trip.
- ❑ Do your taxes if you are going to be gone during tax season.
- ❑ Make photocopies of all your important documents.
- ❑ Purchase your flight ticket.
- ❑ E-mail yourself all important phone numbers, as well as your passport number and have scanned photocopies of passports, driver's license, record of vaccinations etc. in your backpack.

Where in the world should I go?

This is the hardest question you are going to have to make and is completely up to you. Since you do have the entire world to choose from, where do you start?

Look for a general area of the world that you are interested in. Check out a map and look for a logical path that will take you to various countries. You are not limited to staying within the borders of one country.

Anywhere in the world is a possibility. Some spots are more popular than others and each place has something unique to offer. You have the world to choose from.

These areas include:

Asia: Brunei Darussalam, Cambodia, East Timor, India, Indonesia, Laos, Malaysia, Mongolia, Myanmar, Nepal, Philippines, Singapore, Thailand and Vietnam.

Africa: Egypt, Sudan, Libya, Tunisia, Algeria, Morocco, Mauritani, Senegal, The Gambia, Mali, Niger, Burkina Faso, Guinea-Bissau, Guinea, Sierra Leone, Liberia, Côte D'Ivoire, Ghana, Togo, Benin, Nigeria, Cameroon, Equatorial Guinea, São Tomé & Príncipe, Gabon, Congo, Central African Republic, Chad, Congo (Zaire), Rwanda, Uganda, Burundi, Tanzania, Kenya, Somalia, Ethiopia, Djibouti, Eritrea, Madagascar, Mozambique, Malawi, Zambia, Angola, Namibia, Botswana, Zimbabwe, Lesotho, Swaziland, and South Africa.

Oceana: Australia, New Zealand, Japan, Taiwan, and Hong Kong.

Europe: Albania, Andorra, Austria, Belgium, Bosnia-Hercegovina, Britain, Bulgaria, Croatia, Cyprus, Czech

Republic, Denmark, Estonia, Finland, France, Germany, Greece, Hungary, Ireland, Italy, Latvia, Liechtenstein, Lithuania, Luxembourg, Macedonia, Malta, Morocco, Russia, Netherlands, Norway, Poland, Portugal, Romania, St Petersburg, Slovakia, Slovenia, Spain, Sweden, Switzerland, Turkey and Yugoslavia.

Central America: Panama, Costa Rica, Nicaragua, Honduras, El Salvador, Guatemala, and Belize.

South America: Argentina, Bolivia, Brazil, Chile, Colombia, Ecuador, French Guyana, Suriname, Guyana, Paraguay, Peru, Uruguay, and Venezuela.

I have done the Europe and South East Asia areas. All these countries were so close to one another it was easy for me to travel between them. I traveled for more than a year to over thirty countries which would roughly be the size of Canada's two western provinces. My next trips would be the Central and South America route.

If you are still having trouble deciding, here are some questions that you may want to ask yourself:

- ❑ Do I have a specific reason for going?
- ❑ Do I want to find the worlds best party spots?
- ❑ Am I interested art and history?
- ❑ Am I looking for the world's cheapest shopping experience?
- ❑ Do I want to volunteer my services? If so, how?
- ❑ How about learning a new language or skill?
- ❑ Do I want to visit as many countries as possible?
- ❑ Thinking about visiting distant family or relatives?
- ❑ Do I want to teach English as a second language?
- ❑ Do I want to be in a tourist or non-tourist area?

My general rule is to stay away from warring or potentially unstable countries. If you know that one country is planning on attacking another country or there is a possible threat of some sort of disturbance, I advise avoiding that country. I like having the knowledge that I am entering a relatively stable area and don't have to be overly concerned about my personal safety.

Picking the date when you enter into a specific country is also important. Know what to expect if you enter into a country during high or low season. Most of the countries in the world have times when tourists tend to visit. This is high season. Prepare for all the services, the best weather, and the higher prices and more crowds during this time. The low season doesn't usually have the best weather and sometimes there are fewer things to do but there are also fewer tourists and prices are offered at a discount. On the extreme, for some countries tourism completely shuts down during low season. A travel agent or a guidebook would be useful to determine this.

Think about the amount of culture shock you want to experience or think you would enjoy. Culture shock is basically a reaction to a different environment than what you are used to and how you adjust to that difference. Every area of the world offers a different way of living that is unique and different than what you are used to at home. The greater the culture shock, the more chance of finding some amazing adventures and some great stories to take home. If I am going to leave my country, I don't want to end up paying to go to another country similar to my own where I know the food, the culture, and the people. I enjoy countries with exotic environments where I can immerse myself for a while. I would rather go to some foreign hole-in-the-wall eatery than a Western fast food chain.

Talk to other travellers and get their opinions. Some of the best and most accurate information comes from other travellers who have "been there and done that". Walk down to your city's local hostel and meet some experienced backpackers. They are a wealth of knowledge. And, if you are fortunate, you can make some friends and get some contacts in their country.

Go to the library or your local book store and find some travel books on the various countries. Take some time to read through them to find out some specifics and points of interest. A good place to start are books that other backpackers have written regarding their travels.

Note: I have written a companion to this book called: *BACKPACKER: The Journey Begins.* It details the highlights of my travels around the world. A book like that or similar will give you an idea of what the day to day backpacking life style is like.

Search the Internet for specific information. It is easy to get bogged down with too much useless information that is mixed in with the useful. If you have specific questions or need certain information, the Internet is a great tool.

A travel agent is also a great source of information. Usually their information is limited to what they can sell you and many agents may not have personal knowledge of the countries. Most of them have tended to stay only at the resorts and travelled on the package deals. However, they are the source to provide you with the costs of travelling to various countries and other travelling options.

Remember that wherever you go, the place will have its good points and bad points. While you are at home, you are working with imperfect information. One of the great things about backpacking is that you only need a bit of preparation ahead of time before setting out. You can easily do the rest while you are on the road.

Your passport

If there is one thing in all your travelling possessions that I would consider the most invaluable, it would be my passport. A passport is your entry, stay, and exit permit to any destination that is outside your home country.

Without your passport, you will not be able to enter into a new country. The border guards will turn you back until you can present an authentic passport or a passport with a valid visa to enter the country. The guards need to stamp your passport with an entry stamp that includes where you crossed the border and the date.

To exit the country you will need your passport. The border guards will give you an exit stamp next to your entry stamp that proves that you have legally left the country. The guards also will check for the date of the entry stamp on your passport to ensure that you didn't stay longer than you were allowed to.

I am very strict about keeping my passport on my body at all times. Many times, hostels, guesthouses, rental agencies wanted to keep my passport as collateral. This is illegal! Do not let them have it. You can give it to them so they can fill out the necessary forms, but always – ALWAYS – get it back. Place it securely in your money belt which is fastened securely inside your clothes.

In some countries, if you are found without a valid passport on your person, you will be taken to the nearest police station until your identity is proven. This process could sometimes take anywhere from a couple days to a week or longer depending on how strict the security policies of the country are. Some countries are pretty paranoid.

Inside the passport, there is a section where you can fill in your emergency contact information. Ensure that you accurately fill it out. It is also a good idea to contact that person and tell them that you are putting them down as your emergency contact.

As a precaution, photocopy the page in your passport that contains your personal information and picture. Make a couple copies of these and place each of them in a different and secure place in your main pack and day pack. Give a copy to someone you trust back home such as your parents, or close friend.

Take extra passport photos with you – even though color is more expensive, take around a dozen extras. If you are going to enter a country that requires you to get a visa, you will most likely have to produce one or two passport photos along with the application form and money. Having these photos on hand saves you from searching for a photo booth in a foreign country.

If you lose your passport, don't panic. This has happened to other travellers before and there are processes in place to get a new one. Even if you have lost everything, including your money and gear, most embassies and consulates offer financial services to help out in this kind of emergency.

You need to contact your local consulate in the country you are in. This can be found in your guidebook, tourist information centre, or on the Internet. They will inform you about how to obtain a new passport.

Proving your citizenship can be a long process. Your photocopies, identity cards, and birth certificate will help significantly. Once you have proven your identity, you are going to have to wait until your passport is printed in your home country and mailed to you.

The guidebook

Don't leave home without one! I want to emphasize the importance of purchasing a good quality guidebook for your travels. This is one of your essential tools to help you from day to day. There are many quality guidebooks that target different types of travellers. Go through a selection of them and pick out one that meets your needs. Here are the topics that I found important when I travel.

Coverage: Pick a book that covers the country or countries you will be travelling to. I would choose to have a watered down guidebook that covers 10 to 40 counties that I would be travelling to, instead of buying 10 to 30 individual books.

Maps: Detailed, clearly printed maps of all of the major points of interest, roads, and railways are really important. Sometimes this map is all you have when you first arrive in a new place.

City Information: Information on places to stay, things to do, and places to eat. A map of each major city with marked hotels, hostels, restaurants, and points of interest. Also provides a rough estimate of costs and quality for various services.

Quick Facts: Climate, language, currency, visa requirements, costs, dangers, events, etc.

Transportation: What is the best way to move around the country? Listing the various hours of operation, rough estimates of costs, and contact information is useful.

As important a guidebook is in your travels, don't overuse it. Some backpackers fall into the mindset that they will only eat and stay at places that the guidebook lists or go to places the guidebook lists. Use the guidebook while you are in the planning stages for hostels or first arrive in your destination. Your guidebook is just that - a guide - for a traveller to help them decide where to go next and give suggestions on where to stay, what is good to eat, and what to do once they arrive.

The authors of these books can never keep up with all the changes that happen all over the world, nor can they visit every single hostel or restaurant in every city. Once you have a place to stay and know the basic area, head to the tourist agencies or talk to other backpackers for the latest information.

Once you are finished with your guidebook, you have a couple options. You can give it or trade it with another backpacker. I have done this several times. When I was finished with a guidebook, I would see if anyone had another guidebook for the next place I was planning to visit. Most hostels have a "take a book, leave a book" area. Find yourself some other reading material for the trip. You can always keep it and take it home with you. It's sometimes nice to look through it and remember all the places where you have been.

> Note: Some backpackers tear pages out of their guidebooks when they are done with a section or not planning to visit a certain place. I don't do this. I would rather give my book to another backpacker who needs it than destroy it. Also, an undamaged book makes it possible to trade with another backpacker.

Other useful publications

When travelling, there are several books that would be helpful in your day-to-day activities. Just remember before you start purchasing books to bring along, they are something that you are going to have to carry wherever you go and they will take up valuable space in your backpack. They can also be heavy, so choose carefully.

Maps: Maps are the key to getting around in a new area. The maps that are included in the guidebook tend to show only the main streets and half the street names. They are frustrating due to that fact. Free maps of cities are easy to come by at the local tourist agency, hostel/hotel, bus/train station, or Internet café. It is a lot easier to carry around a map of the local area than your bulky guidebook, with an abridged and poorly labelled map.

Language books: Although English is widely spoken in many parts of the world do not assume that everyone speaks it. When travelling to a new country that speaks a different language, it is handy to know some basic phrases. If the locals see that you are trying to speak their language, they usually make an extra effort to help you.

The words that are essential to learn are: “”hello”, “goodbye”, “thank you”, “yes”, “no”, “sorry”, and “welcome”. Knowing the words such as “man”, “woman” and “toilet” are also handy. Most guidebooks have their own small “commonly used words” guide in the back.

Language books are nice, but not essential. If you are going to be spending some time in an area and immerse yourself in the culture, I would recommend one. A small compact pocket version is quite versatile and easy to carry around. Go to your local book store and pick out something that would be practical to use. A language phrase book would most likely be more useful than a language translation dictionary. The phrase book has complete sentences that are designed to be used by travellers, while a dictionary contains translations of words.

Reading Material: If you are ever bored, need to relax and unwind in one spot, or are on a long-haul journey, it is nice to have a small paperback book to read. You only need one and can trade it with other packers when you are done. Limit yourself to focus on one book at a time, to save yourself from carrying around a library in your pack.

Travel insurance

Travel insurance is a must when travelling. Usually your country's medical does not cover you in foreign countries. It's something that we hope never to use, but if something does happen, it is invaluable. Travel insurance can be purchased at any travel agency. Make sure you go over your travel insurance policy carefully with your agent. There are several different types of policies you can get.

Be clear on the limitations of the insurance. If you plan on doing some potentially dangerous activities such as riding a motorcycle, bungee jumping, etc, make sure you are still covered. Some hospitals in some countries will not admit you if you are not covered by insurance. And if you are admitted, the costs of the hospital bills may be a lot more that you can handle.

Some things that I look for:

- Ensure that I am covered completely for my planned length of stay.
- Comprehensive coverage for any hospital stay or emergency transportation back home.
- Ensure I am covered for the countries that I am travelling through.
- Any limitations on the coverage that I am going to receive.

If you can't afford travel insurance, you can't afford to travel.

Inoculations against the nasties

Since we have been brought up in a specific part of the world, we only have immunity to the diseases found in our area. Other countries in the world have different diseases that a foreigner could easily contract. It is best to learn how to minimise the risks and get vaccinated for the areas you are travelling through.

After you have decided where you will be travelling, book an appointment with a local travel nurse. A travel nurse will be able to tell you which vaccinations and medications you will need depending on which regions you are planning to visit.

It's a good idea to do this well in advance as certain vaccinations must be given several months before entering the affected area. Also be sure to obtain your vaccination record, as many countries may turn you away at the border if you cannot prove you have received the correct vaccinations. The nurse will also give you suggestions on how to stay healthy, what to eat, where not to go, and what to do if you do get sick.

In the realm of travel medicine and vaccinations I am a believer of, "If you think that you may need it, but are not sure if it is necessary, spend the extra money and take it." Your travel route may change for some reason or you may be exposed to someone who has been in an infected area. Being sick in a foreign country with questionable medical facilities is not most backpacker's idea of a good time.

If you are on medication, make sure you take enough medicine for the entire trip. Also, have all the contents clearly documented by a doctor – the name of the medicine and dosage as some checkpoints or border guards may be a little suspicious at the contents.

> Note: make sure that you know what drug allergies you have. Hospitals in different countries use different types of drugs. Make sure you know what you can and can't take and make sure that you communicate this to the doctor should the occasion arise. Noting this information on a card in your wallet (translated into a couple of different languages) or wearing a "Medic Alert" bracelet could help you if you're ever in trouble.

Your first aid kit

I was fortunate, in my entire time travelling, I only had to use a couple bandages and some antiseptic. However, it is crucial to have a well-organized medical kit in case of an emergency. Remember, when you're travelling, the majority of the cities and towns have some kind of basic medical centres to help you out.

- ❑ Bandages of various sizes, including "butterfly" bandages
- ❑ Scissors
- ❑ Nail clippers
- ❑ Safety pins
- ❑ Mini sewing kit
- ❑ Multi-vitamins
- ❑ Nutrition bar
- ❑ Waterproof matches
- ❑ Anti-bacterial hand disinfectant
- ❑ Toilet paper
- ❑ Shampoo or all-purpose body wash
- ❑ Glasses or contact lens prescription
- ❑ Emergency feminine hygiene products

While local food is delicious, and street vendors offer a wonderful selection of affordable local food, make sure that it hasn't been sitting in the sun all day. Get things fresh off the grill whenever possible and check to be sure meat has been cooked thoroughly. Trust your instincts. If it looks questionable, don't eat it. It's better to go hungry for a few hours than to suffer from food poisoning in places with less than stellar toilet facilities.

The most important tool in the game of staying healthy while travelling is common sense. Although it is fun to see how the rest of the world lives, I personally have no desire to sample exotic diseases. Stay as clean as possible and listen to the advice of your travel nurse. They will give you guidelines on how to stay healthy. If you feel yourself getting sick or run down, take a few days to relax in your home away from home.

Speaking of toilets, be prepared for anything! Your handy guidebook should detail the proper technique of using a squat, versus a flush toilet. Always have some toilet paper and some hand disinfectant in your backpack because there is no guarantee that you'll find any when nature calls. On the same note, always make sure you have some local currency with you as, in many countries you have to pay a few cents here and there to use the facilities. I learned this the hard way after having a rather desperate and hurried argument with one "toilet guard" in Poland.

What to take

This is what you are going to have to carry with you on your back each time you decide to move. Obviously, the more you pack, the heavier your bag becomes, so you want to pack as little as possible. Backpacks come in various sizes and styles. I have a 72 litre world travel bag with a detachable day pack. With all of my gear packed inside, my pack weighs about 20 pounds and is only half full. Over time, I accumulate a few souvenirs and my pack can weigh as much as 30 to 40 pounds before I mail a box of the things I picked up home.

Your gear is important, so choose wisely. After all, this is the equipment you need to keep you safe and happy for the duration of your journey.

Packsack: Don't skimp on this one. There are many types of bags that you can choose from. My preference is a World Travel Bag. It is specially designed for travellers. It has all the webbing (shoulder, chest, and waist straps) of a normal backpack but can also be transformed into a duffle bag. The main zipper goes all around from the bottom to the top that allows you to lay your pack down and have access to everything without being forced to go through the top or side access areas. There is also a small detachable day pack with shoulder straps that zips onto the main pack.

Have the retail staff select the right size of pack to fit your body. If not, you risk having some pretty uncomfortable moments, not to mention a sore back, shoulders, and waist. Prolonged use of a poorly fitting pack can lead to serious injury. The size of your pack depends on your back length, not your overall height, and since people have different body types, you'll need to find one that suits you. Learn how to use and adjust the straps since they will need to be readjusted occasionally during your travels.

Ask the sales clerk to throw some phone books inside so you can get a feel for what it will be like when it is full of gear. If the suspension (webbing) of your pack is doing its work, most of the packs weight should be transferred to your hips. Before you travel, take some time to break in your pack. Walk around with it on for a while; make sure that it is comfortable.

Guidebook: This is so important that I placed it second in the list. A guidebook (often referred to as the "good book" by packers) is a publication specifically for travellers. It contains information on where to go, what to see, where to sleep, what to eat, what to avoid, how to get there, etc. This is an essential tool that cannot be left at home. Pick your guidebook wisely. I have dedicated a complete section under 'Your guidebook' on how to choose a proper guidebook.

Sarong: A sarong is one of the most versatile items I own. It is a lightweight, rectangular piece of cloth that is the size of a large towel. I use it for a blind fold at night, a towel to dry off with, a blanket for the beach, a head wrap for the sun, a wrap for walking to public showers, a bag for carrying items, a screen for my bunk bed, etc. It dries quickly, is easy to pack, weighs next to nothing, and is easy to clean.

> Note: If you are a man, be careful where you wear one in public. There are many places in the world that are stringent about gender roles and it is foolish or even dangerous to wear anything that will make you stand out in a crowd. Do your research and make sure you don't make yourself a target for any unwanted attention. Always try to blend in with the crowd.

Bathroom kit: This is a special waterproof bag that holds all my necessary toiletries: toothbrush (with a plastic cover for the head), soap (in a plastic container), shaving cream, razor, deodorant, nail clippers, shampoo, exfoliating gloves, contact lens solution, and a comb.

Money Belt: A thin pouch that can be securely strapped inside your clothes, to hold anything valuable. I keep everything that I cannot risk being stolen in there: passport, flight tickets, back-up credit card, photocopies of all important documents, and the bulk of my money. Make sure you get a money belt that breathes (made from cloth) since you will be wearing it next to your body everywhere you go. You keep it on while you are asleep during night and when you are travelling during the day. The only time you take it off is when you wash it.

Note: It is best to keep a small amount of cash in your pockets and everything else in your money belt. In the event that you are mugged, you can simply hand the thief whatever you have in your pockets and hope that he or she won't think to push the matter further. Most money belts are not waterproof, so keep everything that you have inside sealed in a plastic bag.

Wallet: There are travel wallets that attach onto the belt of your pants. It can then be covered by a shirt to keep it out of sight. It is easy to access since you can keep it by your front pocket. Just keep enough money and identification in there for convenience. The majority of your money and identification can be kept in your money belt for extra security. Purses just attract extra attention and should be left at home.

Belt: Not only can you use it to keep your pants up, but you can get ones that have a hidden zipper inside the seam. It's a good place to store spare sets of keys and some emergency coins.

Note: Anything that is not metal and stored in the belt tends to get destroyed. Don't keep your traveller's cheques in there. If there is metal stored in your belt, make sure you take it off when you go through a metal detector.

Pack safe™: This is a wire mesh cover that you can use to keep curious people from exploring your pack when you are not looking. You can use it when you check your luggage on the plane, when walking through crowded stations, or when you have to leave your pack in storage at your hostel. It is slash proof and is a great way of ensuring that the unattended pack without a pack safe™ will get stolen while yours remains safely attached to something immovable. However, it is expensive, heavy, and takes up space in your pack.

Locks: Combination locks are good since you don't have to worry about losing the key but they are next to impossible to open in the dark. When choosing a lock, make sure that you have a couple locks that are small enough to lock your zippers on your packsack together. Get one lock big enough for your Pack safe™ (if you decide to purchase one). When I leave my pack unattended, I lock my zippers into my Packsafe™ mesh so that no one can move the zippers apart and reach through the mesh to get inside my pack.

Jacket: A high quality, properly designed, weather resistant jacket is important. I look for several things in a good jacket. I prefer to have one that is made from Gore-tex™. Gore-Tex™ is expensive material but it is waterproof and, more importantly, it breathes, which means that you don't have to worry about getting soaked in your own sweat.

All the jackets main pockets should be accessible from the outside and should have zippers or Velcro™ fasteners Big pockets are a plus since I usually carry my wallet, sunglasses, camera, gloves, and emergency food in my jacket. A detachable hood is also a nice feature when you get caught in a rainstorm. Pit zips, or zipable vents under the arm pits are great for increasing air flow. A zip-in inner fleece is handy to have since you can remove it or put it in whenever you want.

Note: I purchased a BMW Bomber jacket in Singapore. It looked good but when it started raining, I got soaked and cold. It was impractical but fashionable. I switched to a three ply Gor-tex™ outdoor jacket. This jacket was able to keep me dry and warmer in any weather. Being comfortable and safe with the right choice of clothes is an important part of travelling. You are going to be relying on your gear to keep you alive and well.

Pants: I prefer taking a pair of cotton pants with zip-off legs. They are made out of a durable cotton fabric that is light, water repellent, and can dry within an hour. You are able to unzip the pants just above the knees and turn them into shorts.

The pockets with zippers or Velcro™ on them help keep things safe and are easy to roll up into a ball and store in your pack. I tend to go with darker colors. When they get dirty it is less noticeable. I find blue jeans are too heavy to pack, uncomfortable to wear in hot climates and take too long to dry when they get wet.

Shirts: A basic cotton t-shirt is great to have. You can sleep with it on during the night or use it solo on a hot day or in a layer with warmer clothes when you are in a colder environment. Do some research on the environment that you will be staying in and use common sense when picking out your clothes.

Long sleeve fleece shirt: Fleece is great for keeping the heat in and is completely breathable so you won't sweat as easy. It is great to wear with just an over shirt, or layered with a Gor-tex™ shell jacket. Remember to try to keep your fleece dry, and if it does get wet, take time to dry it out. It is not very wind resistant and a cool breeze can quickly suck the heat out of your fleece.

> Note: A rolled fleece shirt can also substitute for a pillow in times when you don't want to use the one provided for you.

Bathing suit: Even if you are not going in the summer time or near any beaches, it's good to have a bathing suit along. There are times when I relaxed in the local aquatic centre. If you have swimming trunks, they can double as a pair of shorts.

Femine hygiene products: If you are a woman, make sure you take an extra supply of these products in your bag. Don't forget, you can restock almost anywhere in the world.

Waterproof bag cover: You can get a waterproof cover for your packsack. When you are outside with your pack and it is raining, you can cover it with this light bag to ensure the contents stay dry. I also use it for taking a shower. Instead of leaving my personal effects (passport, wallet, keys, towel, and clothes) hanging up outside in the open, I bring everything into the shower with me and place them in the waterproof bag. And I don't have to worry about anyone taking my gear or it getting wet in the shower.

Photocopies: The overall idea is to have a backup of any documents or ID that are important for the trip. Send yourself an e-mail to your Internet web mail of any important information and make photocopies of all important documents. Try to fit everything on one or two pages. Even though these are copies, the information contained is still valuable and sensitive. Place the photocopies in various places throughout your gear. I had a total of three sets: one went in a zip lock bag in my money belt, the second was in my main pack in my utility bag, and the third was hidden in a compartment in my day pack.

Make sure that you copy:

- Passport
- Identity card
- Drivers license and international drivers license
- Credit cards
- Bank cards
- Travel insurance
- Medical cards
- Inoculation list
- Emergency contact names and phone numbers

Shoes and sandals: Make sure you have a good pair of walking shoes and that you break them in before you leave. You will be wearing them every single day so make sure that they are comfortable and suitable for any sort of terrain you might come across. Sandals can be used in the outdoors and even inside the hostels while showering.

Sleep sheet: Sometimes when it is necessary to sleep in a bed that you believe could be a bit questionable, using a sleep sheet is a good idea. It is a sheet the length of your body that has the side and bottom sewn together. It is effectively a silk or cotton barrier between you and the sheets on the bed. You can buy a cotton or silk sleep sheet or make your own. Just take a regular flat sheet from your bed and sew the bottom and side up. You now have your very own sleep sheet.

Note: Some hostels require you to have a sleep sheet. If you don't have one, you may have to rent one for the duration of your stay. Save money and bring your own.

Compass: It is a good idea to have a compass, as well as a good map, while travelling. Take the time to learn how to use it properly, or you may as well cut down on the weight and leave it at home. Most backpackers don't use compasses but I became a compass addict and used mine extensively.

Sunglasses: Get a good pair with at least UVA and UVB 400 protection. I would strongly advise a decent pair of sunglasses. The knock offs look good but they could end up hurting your eyes in the long run. Keeping them in a clamshell case helps protect them from getting bent or broken.

Glasses and contact lenses: If you wear contacts, make sure you carry at least one full bottle of each type of solution with you. Most places in the world carry solutions for various types of contacts, but sometimes it requires a little searching in an unknown country. If you do wear contacts, have a backup pair in your money belt.

If you wear glasses, it is also a good idea to have a back up pair just in case. Use a hard clamshell case when storing them in your pack.

Vitamins and energy bars: Always have a supply of full spectrum multi-vitamins and emergency energy bars on hand. It's wise to take your multi-vitamins daily as it's hard to gauge the nutritional value of some of the food you'll be getting.

Flashlights: I am a big fan of the LED headlamp. It is small, powerful, and comes with a headband, allowing you to have both hands free. It is also lightweight, energy efficient, and will save you valuable space in your pack. There are some waterproof head lamps that you can get. A regular flashlight is usually bigger and heavier but gives a brighter beam of light and lasts a bit longer.

Birth control: It's smart to be careful when you are travelling. If you are planning on being sexually active or if there is a small chance that an encounter could happen, be prepared. If you are going to have sex, use the proper protection. Not only will it prevent an unplanned pregnancy, but will help to prevent you from getting sexually transmitted diseases.

Utility kit: I have a bag of items that I use on occasion. They include: a small first aid kit (the suggested contents are in the 'My first-aid kit' section of this book) sewing kit, super glue, multipliers/Swiss army knife, lighter, candle, sunscreen, bug repellent, and spare batteries.

Camera: Even though digital cameras are more expensive than 35mm cameras, I would still recommend choosing digital. You can burn your pictures to CD in nearly every country in the world and you don't have to worry about buying film. If you bring your digital camera, make sure that you have your cables and driver software with you.

Necklace key chain: Instead of putting keys in your pockets, buy a neck strap and put your keys on that. It is easy to find your keys. They're also out of the way, and much harder to steal.

Wristwatch with alarm: Get a digital wristwatch with an alarm and backlight instead of a travel clock. They come in handy when you have a schedule to keep or when you need to take a nap at the train station and should wake up in x minutes. I have a Timex™ Datalink watch which stores some of my emergency telephone numbers and important dates. It has up to ten individual alarms you can set and two time zone settings.

Journal: I would highly recommend you get one and keep it up to date. It is amazing what you forget if you don't write it down right away. A journal takes time to write, but when you are looking back on your adventures, it is nice to see what you have done and who you have met. Also along the way, you are going to start collecting other backpackers' contact information and e-mail addresses. Keeping it all in your journal makes it easier than trying to keep track of napkins and stray bits of paper.

Hostelling International (HI) Card: This card will allow you to stay at HI Hostels around the world. The Hostel Association has a website (http://www.hihostels.com/openHome.sma) where you can go to find out which countries have hostels that will recognize this card. Do your homework. In certain parts of the world an HI card can save you a lot of money and in other places it will be virtually useless.

Student card: If you are a student, bring your International Student Identity Card (ISIC). It will save you a lot of money on admission and events in many places around the world. I have heard of lots of backpackers "obtaining" student cards in the streets of Bangkok.

Bank (ATM) card: Your bank card should work nearly anywhere in the world. Just make sure that it is affiliated with the international banking systems such as Curris™, Interac™, Visa™, etc. Be careful of variable service charges and exchange rates in different countries. There have been bank machines that are known to 'eat' bank cards. Just make sure you have a spare handy.

Credit card: Great to have and accepted nearly anywhere. Take a good look at what your credit card's extra features offer you. Many times you can get travel insurance, as well as product insurance on your purchases.

Emergency food: Non-perishable, well-sealed food for when you don't have a chance to eat. I go with a couple high end energy bars or some energy gel. Experiment before you leave to see which brands you like the best.

Earplugs: For those times when you need to get that good night's sleep and there is a person snoring in the bunk above you. Take a couple pairs in case you lose one or if they get dirty. You can pick these up at a local pharmacy, but they are cheaper at the hardware stores.

CD/MP3 player and book: Books are good since you are able to trade with other packers and lots of hostels have a section called "Take a book. Leave a book." A CD/MP3 player is great but it does use up a steady supply of batteries and you'll feel terrible if it gets stolen.

Deck of playing cards: It's a great way to meet other backpackers, and it helps to pass long hours of travel time on the bus or train.

Jewellery: In general, don't bother. It's an unnecessary nuisance and an attraction for thieves. Make sure your watch is not an expensive one. Anything that makes you look better off than the locals is bound to get you unwanted attention. Women, however, might consider wearing a wedding band, especially in many South American and Arabic countries where single women are much more likely to get hassled than those who are supposedly married.

Pins: Get a handful of pins of your countries flag. It is a really nice gesture to give someone a pin like this. Each time I ran low, I went to my consulate to get another handful.

Overall, when you are packing, remember to focus on function over fashion. You can still look good by just packing the basics. When at home, there is a lot of pressure to be "in fashion". When you are travelling overseas, you don't have to care too much about this. It's more important to blend in with the locals and be comfortable than be on the cutting edge fashion from your home country. I strongly suggest that you choose function over fashion.

Remember, people all over the world wear clothes. Shocking, I know, but it is true. This means that they have stores that sell clothes. Sometimes you can buy the same thing for a lot less than what you would pay for it at home. Also, they have various supplies that you can buy at the stores. There is no need to take a bunch of tubes of toothpaste, extra sunscreen lotion, or even a stockpile of bar soap.

Buy it on the road, I purposely under pack whenever I can. If I know that I can get the same thing cheaper when I arrive at my destination, I don't bother to pack it. Replenish your supplies as you go.

How much to take

We have a tendency to over pack when travelling for the first time since you have no idea what to expect overseas and want to prepare for anything that could possibly happen to you. Unfortunately, you have a limited amount of space in your backpack and you are going to have to carry it on your back wherever you go. The more you put into a backpack, the more it is going to weigh and the less space you have. The goal is to pack only the essential gear and keep your pack as light as possible.

There is no rule that you have to fill your pack to capacity. I like to leave around 10% to 20% of my pack empty in case I decide to pick something up. Pack only what you need and leave the rest.

The total weight of your pack is important. When you are on the road, you will have this backpack strapped to you for sometimes hours on end. There have been occasions where I had to run with my pack on to catch a bus or train. Sometimes, finding a place to stay requires walking through various urban terrains such as stairs, tunnels, pedestrian ways, etc. Trust me, a light pack will help you enjoy your trip.

The amount of clothes you take with you should be minimal. Pack for your environment, not for fashion.

Note: If you are heading to a place in Asia such as Bangkok or Korea, only pack one change of clothes. While you are there you can go on a shopping spree and buy everything at a quarter of the price it is back home.

Half and half again: Take all of your clothes you are planning on taking and lay them out on your bed. Now, select half of them (50%) and get rid of the rest. Now that you have made the tough decision of removing half of your clothes, do it again. Of the remaining 50% take half of them away again. Now you are getting down to what should be packed in your packsack. If you think that you can get rid of half again, do so. You are now left with a small pile of clothes that will fit into your backpack.

My 5 x 5 x 2: This means five t-shirts, five socks/underwear and two pairs of pants. I travelled like this for over a year and had no problems. This was the majority of my clothing. I also had one fleece long sleeve shirt and a bathing suit. Over time, I did lose or wreck some clothes, but I just replaced them as I travelled.

Note: By using the inside out method (wear certain articles of clothing inside out) it gives you approximately double the number of days before you have to do laundry.

Put on your pack by yourself: Sometimes you don't have the luxury of getting someone to help you with your packsack. If you need help getting your pack on or struggle in lifting it, seriously think about reducing its weight.

One arm it: I want to be able to lift my pack with one arm. There have been many times when I had to grab my pack and throw it on my back in crowded areas or when my other arm was holding something else.

Imagine that you are at a bus stop and your bus pulls up on the other side of the street. You have to grab your pack and run over to board the bus before it leaves. There has been more than one time where I have had to grab my pack with one arm, swing it over my shoulder and ran to catch that bus.

Packing it

There are several ways of packing and sorting everything in your pack. Let me share a method that works well for me. I sort my clothes in different coloured plastic bags. I have a shirt bag, a bag for socks and underwear, a bag for pants, a utility equipment bag, and a laundry bag. The bags keep everything together and keep your stuff dry when your pack gets wet. My utility bag is the heaviest and least used, so it goes to the bottom of my pack. On top of that, I place my laundry bag which fills up as the days go on and then my pants' bag which I only use once or twice a week. On top of the laundry and pants' bag, I have my underwear, and shirt bags. These are used at least once every two days. Loose at the top of the pack is my Pack Safe™, bathroom kit, sarong, travel food, and long sleeve fleece shirt.

I like this method for easily keeping everything together and to waterproof my gear.

For small items that need to be protected from water, place them in a zip-loc bag. All of the contents in my money belt, and photocopied identification, were in such a bag. Take some extras in case the ones that you are using break.

Main pack or day pack: What should I place in my day pack and what should I place in my main pack? The day pack should contain everything you need for that time when your main pack is not accessible. Again, focus on just the essentials that you are going to need that day.

The only time I detach my day pack from my main pack is when I jump on the bus and my main pack is in the storage compartment on the bus. I don't bother wearing a day pack when I am in a populated city. I want to blend in as much as possible with my environment and not look like a tourist. Everything I need is in my zipped up pockets in my jacket and pants.

> Note: Imagine that you lose your main pack. What do you need in your day pack to hold out for a few days before you recover you main pack?

Test it out: Now that you have everything all packed in your backpack, carry it around the house for a few hours. Walk up and down some stairs, go outside, and practice taking it off and putting it on without assistance. This is your true "break in" period.

What to do with your money

The amount of money you are going to need when travelling is an important question to ask and a hard question to accurately answer. The amount depends on how long you are going to be travelling, what you are going to be doing, and how much you intend to spend while you're on the road.

Do some research in your guidebook and on the Internet to find out the range of prices you will be encountering. Make sure you convert the currency to something you understand to get a good estimate. Knowing how much you are going to spend before you go will help you know how much money you are going to have to save. It is always good to have a bit more for emergencies and to have some to come home to.

You will spend money every day on your accommodation and eating. Wherever you travel you will have to pay for transportation. You may have to pay for a visa to cross into a country. The rest are your more optional expenses that can be moderated. Purchasing items for yourself and others or using services such as the Internet or phone are small costs but will add up over time. Taking a course or paying an entrance fee for a museum or exhibition will also drain your funds. A night of drinking and socializing has the potential of being costly.

Some countries require that you have and can prove that you have a specific amount of money in your bank account before they let you into the country. Do some research ahead of time.

I use two separate bank accounts to draw money from and each account has its own bank (ATM) and credit card. One account is my primary that I draw on for the majority of my funds, the second account is for an emergency backup (again, with its own bank and credit card). I do this for two reasons.

The first being that if I lose one set of cards, I have backups in my money belt. Secondly, if I run out of money on my primary account, I know I either have to find more money or cut my travelling short since I am pulling from my emergency account.

Travellers' cheques used to be the way to go before the invention of the bank card. I do take travellers' cheques but as a last resort or 'I need money now' cases.

Emergency money on hand is also important to have. Figure out how much the following would cost: You are stuck in the middle of nowhere and need to get transportation ($) to a hotel for the night ($), a quick meal ($) and then a trip to the airport ($). Take this amount and have it on you at all times and keep it in your money belt. If you loose everything, you still have enough to get you a meal, shelter and a trip to the airport.

Your itinerary – not needed

Before we leave, it sometimes makes us feel better if we have a plan for which countries we are planning to visit, what to see, and how long we are going to stay. That way we know we can see everything we want to see, and have the security of knowing what we are going to do the next day. We can make sure all of our rooms are booked ahead of time and a cab waiting for us at our arrival point. Keeping to a schedule ensures we don't miss anything that we want to see.

That's great. Don't do it.

For some people, not knowing where they are going to sleep the next night or which city they are going to be in the next day is a frightening step into the unknown. Some cannot even fathom the idea of not creating a day to day plan of a trip. It takes a little courage and some experience before you realize that you do not need to plan everything in advance. If you must plan, make it rough, on paper, and in pencil. That way you can easily make changes or throw it out.

Over the course of my travels, I met up with hundreds of other backpackers and found a general commonality on how they all planned their trip.

They don't!

Everyone has a general idea of the direction where they are going and how long they are going to be travelling. Beyond that, most of the planning happens the day before when they feel its time to leave their current spot.

The reason for this is that you do not know what a place has to offer until you get there. Travel guides, the Internet, and word of mouth are great ways of finding out if the city could be of interest to you before you arrive. But the accuracy and coverage of these places is sometimes quite limited and potentially out of date. Also, the amount of work required to research this is cumbersome and not usually worth your while. The best laid plans are those made up when you arrive in the city and walk into the local tourist agency or hostel.

When you first start backpacking, it takes a week or two of "on the road" time travelling to different areas before you lose your need to 'have a room reserved for you, and a taxi waiting for you at the train station'. You realize how easy it is to travel on the spur of the moment and how limiting an itinerary really is.

I do not usually plan for more than a day or two in advance. However, I do have a plan of a general route that I follow around the world, and which countries I want to visit. This is mainly to avoid back-tracking. Beyond that, I have no clue what is going to happen or what I am going to do.

Keep in mind your route and plan are not set in stone. It will change and evolve as you go to different places, talk to locals, and find out from other backpackers what is "cool" to see and do. This is the making for numerous side-trips. You have a choice to make: should you throw away your precious schedule or do something that interests you? Basically, when you come to a new place, if you like it, stay a little longer, if you hate it, just leave the following day and go somewhere else. No worries!

Note: Some of my greatest times have been when I found something new and changed my timetable or when I met someone who would take me to an interesting place. There may be a concert or an event that you discover which may require a 'detour' of a couple days.

Internet tools before travelling

The Internet is an excellent tool for gathering important information before you leave your country. I have listed what I found useful while researching backpacking and future destinations. At the end of each section, I have placed an Internet link to either an online directory, Internet keyword search, or a direct link to a web page. The Internet directory is the best way to go, it is like an online yellow pages and provides an up-to-date list of all known websites on that subject. The Internet search keywords are suggestions on what you can type into a search engine like: http://www.google.com, http://www.yahoo.com, etc. If I couldn't find what I needed to know with an Internet directory or keyword search, I provide the address of the website.

Guidebooks: Most guidebooks publishers have their own website. Information in your book is always changing and any updates will be on the site. Also, they are a great reference for some initial research on what is offered in the country, and other useful facts. Many of them publish a newsletter that is sent weekly, monthly or annually. Some of the better ones offer free news groups where anyone can ask a question and it is answered by fellow backpackers.

Internet Search Directories:
http://directory.google.com/Top/Recreation/Travel/Specialty_Travel/Backpacking/

http://directory.google.com/Top/Recreation/Travel/Specialty_Travel/Budget/

DFAIT: DFAIT is the Department for Foreign Affairs and International Trade. This is the government's lifeline to all travellers. It has a wealth of information on what is currently happening in a particular country as it relates to your nationality. I check any travel advisories (which tend to be a bit overly conservative for my taste, but they are just covering all the bases), visa requirements, maximum length of stay permitted, etc. If you are going to be staying long in a particular country, you can register yourself with your country's consulate and have them keep tabs on you.

Internct Search Keywords:
dfait + {the name of your country}

Website address:
http://www.embassyworld.com/

E-mail: There are many free e-mail websites on the Internet and all can be accessed from any Internet terminal around the world. E-mail allows you to stay in touch with your old friends and family and also your new friends that you are going to be making while travelling. Some packers create a special e-mail address just for travelling and give it out freely to whomever wants it. They have a primary one that they keep to themselves.

When you meet other backpackers, the preferred method to stay in touch is to exchange e-mail addresses. In the back of my journal I have a list of e-mails that I collected. I found it useful to make sure I have their full name and a small description of them. After a while, you get a name: Xe' Chi – madfish@e-mailaddress.com and have no idea who the person is.

Some people like to protect their privacy when travelling. They would get a temporary account such as: carltravelstheworld@e-mailaddress.com. This way, after you get home and given your e-mail address to a thousand or so strangers, you can pick who you want to give your real e-mail address to.

Internet Search Directories:
http://directory.google.com/Top/Computers/Internet/E-mail/Free/Web-Based/

http://dir.yahoo.com/Business_and_Economy/Business_to_Business/Communications_and_Networking/Internet_and_World_Wide_Web/E-mail_Providers/Free_E-mail/

Blogging: A blog is basically a web log or an online diary that anyone with an Internet connection can create and update. Anyone, or only people whom you specify can read what you are writing and post their comments to each of your entries. There are many free services on the Internet that offer these services. This is the best way to stay in touch, since your friends would come and read what you are writing whenever they want to without you filling up people's e-mail box with your periodic ramblings.

Internet Search Directories:
http://directory.google.com/Top/Computers/Internet/On_the_Web/Weblogs/Tools/Publishers/

http://dir.yahoo.com/Computers_and_Internet/Internet/World_Wide_Web/Weblogs/Software/

http://dir.yahoo.com/Society_and_Culture/Cultures_and_Groups/Cyberculture/Virtual_Communities/

The flight tickets

Air fares are not all alike. This is one of your biggest outlays of cash and it happens before you start travelling. Understanding the differences and options can save you a lot of money. Take some time to shop around for the best deal and don't be afraid to ask questions regarding the stipulations on your flight. Travel agents are a good source of knowledge on which areas are popular, some basic do's and don't's and what is on sale the time of year you are planning to travel.

Student airfares: Having an International Student Identity Card (ISIC) with the right flight agency will allow you to get on board at a student price or take advantage of a student package. The great deal with these fares, besides being cheaper, is that they are tailor-made for backpackers. They allow you to be flexible if you need to change your flight dates (sometimes you have to pay a small processing fee), purchase your seat in advance and have no minimum stay. Sometimes you are allowed to stay up to one year without paying additional money.

Published and negotiated fares: These are your regular flights between two established destinations that are serviced by a variety of airlines. You are able to shop around for the best ticket by comparing the different airlines. Check the restrictions on these tickets carefully. Sometimes you are limited to the length of your stay, your ability to change the flight dates, the number of days before you are able to cancel or even get a refund on your ticket, etc.

Seat sales: These are unpredictable and, in most cases, have blackout periods. A blackout period is a restriction on when you are able to fly. The price of the ticket is heavily discounted, but at awkward times. In most cases, you will have to book a ticket well in advance and don't have much of a chance at a refund or changing the dates.

Charter fares: These are seasonal fares to popular destinations. With more people travelling to one spot more often the fares are lower. The choice of destinations is a little limiting and usually has quite strict restrictions on baggage, cancellations, flight dates, and changes. These are first come, first served and the price will vary depending on demand and availability, meaning that each flight could sell out completely or not at all.

Stopovers are good to have when travelling as a backpacker. A stopover is where you have to disembark your plane, and wait for another one to continue on your journey. It adds time and the stress of being herded around a strange airport and waiting for your next plane to depart. Airlines try to give regular passengers the luxury of having the least amount of stopovers before they get to their destination.

And so, why are stopovers good? You can ask for a longer stopover at your destination. This means that when you fly to your ultimate destination, you have an opportunity to travel to another country (your stopover) for free! Sometimes you can have a stopover as long as one year before you have to continue on to your next destination.

Note: If you are stopped at immigration and they ask you how long you are planning on staying in a country and your ticket says that you are going to be a year, you may have some problems. It is best to set the length of the stop over to just under your maximum limit of when you are allowed to visit. When you are in the country (with the stamp in your passport), extend your stop over to as long as you want. To renew your stamp on your passport, just cross the border into a new country, and when you eventually come back, you get a new stamp for another maximum number of days.

Internet Search Directories:
http://directory.google.com/Top/Recreation/Travel/Transportation/Air/Budget_Airfares/

Website address:
http://www.ryanair.com
http://www.easyjet.com

On the road

Introduction

You have finally made it into your first country……What do you do now? This entire section is dedicated to providing the much needed first steps in travelling. Usually it takes around two weeks or so of trial and error, during which time you make it up as you go along. These are all the lessons I learned while travelling. You are going to refine all these suggestions to your own liking as you progress. Near the end of my travels, I was able to pass on a lot of my experience to first time travellers. I started to realize that what I was doing had become a habit, and was not necessarily common knowledge to everyone.

When my plane touched down at my first foreign country I was making it up as I went along. I was relying on the advice my travelling buddy found on the Internet a couple months prior on where to stay. We went up to a bank machine and had no idea how much local currency to get out – 10, 100, 1000, 10000 Bhatt. Without a map, but with some crudely waved directions from the cab driver we started walking towards the guesthouse area. Is this the right area of town for backpackers?

We were able to compare prices and compare some accommodations. Were we paying too much? What makes this a good place to stay? Should we be looking for something else? Eventually selecting a place and stuffing our packs in our room, we then had no idea what to do after that. Where are the good places to visit? We walked around without a map, since we didn't know where the maps were to see if we could find anything of interest. Surely there were places in the city where we should not go, some scams that we should be aware of? Sure there were, but where do we find that information?

This section is to answer these questions and make your first backpacking experience much. It assumes that you have just touched down at your destination.

Jet lag and culture shock

You have just crossed several times zones and landed in a new exotic country on the other side of the planet. Even though the sun may be high in the sky and your watch may tell you it's the middle of the afternoon, your body may be telling you that you should be sleeping in bed. Not only will your body be adjusting to the new sleeping, waking, and eating schedules, you are also going to adapt to a completely new environment. There could be huge altitude changes, climate changes, and cultural changes to deal with.

Jet lag is your body adjusting to a new time zone. Our bodies are designed for regular cycles of daylight and darkness, this is referred to as our circadian rhythm. Crossing time zones forces your body to change its expected awake and sleep schedules. You begin to feel symptoms like daytime drowsiness, difficulty sleeping, and general fatigue. People have been known to experience a form of jet lag by crossing as little as three time zones. Jet lag only happens when you fly east or west crossing time zones. If you are flying north or south, you wouldn't experience any jet lag.

I flew from Singapore (+30 degrees Celsius) to Calgary (-20 degrees Celsius and ten hours difference) to Madrid (+5 degrees Celsius and eight hours difference) within a month. I was feeling the effects of jet lag and climate shock for a couple of weeks. I didn't know when I was tired, when I was hungry, or when I needed to use the toilet.

There are ways of dealing with and limiting the effects of jet lag.

Before you leave:

- Avoid alcohol and caffeine before you board the plane. Don't go out on a drinking binge and get yourself plastered the night before. Having artificial depressants or stimulants in your system will not help your body adjust when you land. Needless to say, waking up with a hangover is never a pleasant thing.
- Make sure you get a good rest.
- Wear comfortable, non-constricting clothes and shoes while on the plane. This will help with blood circulation.
- Have a meal that is high in starches, carbohydrates, and greens.

When you are in the plane:

- Set your watch to reflect the time in your destination country. This helps you to adjust to your new sleep schedule.
- Try to eat your in-flight meals based on the time of day in your destination country.
- Walk around in the cabin or do some stretching.
- Stay hydrated, try to drink a glass of water each hour.
- Sleep on the plane based on the time in your destination country.
- Put something over your eyes to simulate darkness.
- Stay relaxed, try to enjoy your flight.

When you arrive:

- Do your best to stay awake during the day and not take a nap. This will help with the insomnia when you are trying to sleep at night.
- Eat when the locals eat. Try to adjust to their eating schedule as soon as possible.
- Try not to snack at night.

Depending on where you land, you are going to be dealing with culture shock. Simply put, you are going to be arriving in a new land, with new cultures and ideas, and it's going to take some adjustment for you to get used to this new environment. Most backpackers experience some kind of culture shock when they initially arrive in a foreign country.

When you first enter into a new country, everything is new and exciting. You enjoy absorbing all the new experiences that are offered to you. After a while, the newness wears off and you start to discover minor irritations and annoyances. It could be as simple as not being able to communicate or eating new foods. This is basically you transitioning from your previous ways of doing things to your new culture.

Some of the symptoms are:

- Longing for your family back at home.
- An unwillingness to interact with the new culture.
- Anger, resentment, and changes in temperament.
- You start to stereotype the new culture.
- Feeling of insecurity or inadequacy.

The good news is that there are ways of coping with culture shock.

- Be patient and don't try too hard.
- Maintain a little contact with your ethnic group and your new culture.
- Learn to be constructive, be positive and celebrate the little things.
- Introduce some form of exercise or physical activity.
- Start learning about the new culture, try picking up part of the language.
- Find a place to relax and unwind if feeling stressed.
- Accept the new country as it is. Don't complain, just accept.

Note: One of the best things about being a backpacker, if you really don't like a place, you can always go someplace else that is nearby.

Each time I arrive

You grab your pack from the luggage area and set foot for the first time in some new strange place. What do you do now?

Many of us have termed this: "The Struggle". When you arrive at a new place, you have no idea where anything is located, what it is going to be like, or even if you are going to enjoy what the place has to offer. It may be raining outside or getting dark and you need to somehow find a place to stay for the night. Finding accommodation is my first and only priority when I arrive in a new place. Everything else is secondary and can wait until after I have my room for the night. The last thing I want to do is be in a strange city without a place to sleep safely and store my pack.

Locate accommodations: You are first confronted with a choice: either find the local tourist agency or use your guidebook's map to find the area where the backpacker accommodations are located.

Tourist agencies are preferable since they have the latest accurate information that is relevant to you. There are a couple of ways to find out where the tourist agencies are located. The first is to consult your guidebook. If there is a tourist agency in the area, your guidebook would definitely have it. Tourist information is usually located in or next to a train station, airport or bus station. The international symbol for tourist information is a green or blue circle with a lower case 'i' in the middle. If you still can't find it, you can always ask someone for directions. If you do choose to go to the tourist agency, travel there as fast as you can. You will be competing for rooms with all of the other tourists and backpackers who have also just arrived.

At the tourist agency, you can ask for a free map of the local area and where the budget hostels are. The maps in your guidebook are very much watered down and do not show all the street names. The tourist agency map is usually a better map that can easily be folded up and stored in your pocket.

Most of the time, the tourist agencies have a list of places to stay in the city complete with phone numbers, addresses and prices. This is usually more up to date and comprehensive than your guidebook. The tourist agency can also phone around for you and check for room availability and rates. Sometimes, for a small fee, they can reserve you a room while you walk over to your accommodation. This is a nice feature during high season when the budget hostels tend to get filled up quite quickly.

You can always use the map from your guidebook to find the inexpensive hostels. Often they have descriptions and contact information for the few hostels they checked out. This list is not complete or accurate since the book was most likely published a year or so prior, and a lot of things can change: prices, contact numbers, hostel closures/openings, etc.

If your guidebook doesn't have a map or a write up of the local area, and you can't find the tourist agency, there are still places that can help you. If you can, find the most expensive hotel in the city, I prefer a three star or higher, and ask for a map of the city. Even though you are not staying at the hotel, more often than not, they will give you a map for free and give directions on how to get to the inexpensive hostels.

Often the locals will try to help the best that they can, but the knowledge of the "cheapest hotel" may escape them. They have never bothered to stay in a hotel in their own city. They can probably point you to a nearby hotel, but it most likely will not be the cheapest.

As the last resort, you can try ask a local, a tout, or take a taxi, but this is sometimes a little risky. A taxi driver is motivated to make money so sometimes they take advantage of the fact that you are a foreigner in their city. They can do this one of two ways, either drive you around for a bit and inflate the fare, or take you to a hostel or inexpensive hotel that gives them a commission. Always insist on having the cab driver use the meter. A lot of the time, when they say, "good price for you", it actually means, "good income for me."

A tout is a person hired to find tourists and backpackers and direct them to a list of hotels that pay them commission. They sometimes will put you on the right transportation and call ahead and reserve a room for you. This sounds great but you are going to pay for the extra service. If you ask for a hostel that is not on their list, they will tell you (may insist) that the hostel is either full or not good to stay at. Translation: Why would I put you in a hostel that doesn't pay me any commission?

I avoid taking taxis and using touts if I can.

On the way to the area, I always try to notice and read all the signs and shops that I pass. You are going to have to come back this way when you leave. And if you are going to be staying in this part of town, it is nice to get a feel for the neighbourhood and what services are offered and any points of interest.

Choose a place: Once you find the hostel area, walk around. Budget hostels are usually grouped close together in certain sections of towns. It is convenient to walk to a couple of them and compare prices and standards and pick the one that is best suited to your liking.

Check in: When I decide to check into a hostel, I usually pay for two nights on the first day. That way, I am not worried about losing my room the next day and can sleep in if I am tired. If they ask for my passport, I let them have it to take down the relevant information but I always make sure I get it back. I never let it out of my sight.

Get a bed: I prefer to sleep on the lower bunk in a dorm room. If, for some reason, I have to get up in the middle of the night, I don't want to have to find that little ladder to climb down to the floor in the dark.

Secure my gear: From the top of my packsack I take out my sarong, Packsafe™, waterproof bag, bathroom kit, and sleep sheet. Using Packsafe™, I lock all of my zippers to the Packsafe™ mesh and wrap the entire wire mesh around and secure it to my bed. I throw on the water proof bag around my packsack and slide it under my bed if possible or under the sheets. That way my pack looks like a big back blob and is wrapped up in a steel mesh attached onto an immovable object. I take my sarong and attach it to the bottom of the top bunk, effectively creating a curtain. More often than not, my sarong is still damp from using it as a towel that morning and needs to dry out. Lastly, I unroll my sleep sheet on the bed and stick my shaving kit under my pillow for later use that night. This entire process takes me around five minutes.

Small walkabout: I then take a walk around the neighbourhood. I like to get a feel of my new surroundings. I don't go very far, just enough to know where some of the major routes are, pick out some points of interest, and generally familiarize myself with the local area. If there is a grocery store near by, I stock up on some groceries for the next few days.

Socialize: When I arrive back at the hostel, I go to the common area or kitchen to quickly make some friends and hang out for a bit. Other backpackers are great to hang out with, and, those that have been there for a few days, can give you some valuable pointers on some good places to check out.

Where to stay

You are now in a new city so your first concern is finding a place to sleep and store your pack. With a wide range of choices, what works best for a backpacker on a budget? If I had a choice between a couple of places, what should I look for? Here is a list of the possibilities starting with the least expensive.

On the night train/bus: Save the cost of a night's accommodation and go to sleep on the night train or bus while you are going to your next destination. There were many times when I opted for the cheaper night bus or train so I could wake up at my new destination. Sleeping on trains is usually easier than sleeping on the bus. There is more leg room, you are not in the middle of traffic, and sometimes you have your own compartment. Just make sure that your gear is secured someplace safe.

Friend's place: This is definitely the best accommodation that you can receive. Not only is it free and comes equipped with all the living needs, you have a local person who can show you were to go and what to do. Since this is their home, they want to show you the best of it.

Free accommodations: There are such things in this world. There are online services that allow backpackers to freeload with other people around the world. There is no monetary, sexual or any other obligation. However, everything is not guaranteed and just use your common sense before you decide to stay at someone's place.

Internet Search Directories:
http://directory.google.com/Top/Recreation/Travel/Lodging/Hospitality_Clubs/?il=1

Camping: Nearly every destination has camping facilities that are located on the outskirts of town. You get your plot of land to set up your tent and a place to cook (usually a fire pit). Showers and stores are usually located on the grounds and are available for a fee. You are away from most of the hustle and bustle of the city. These are great places to unwind and relax. Some of the bigger campgrounds have common rooms for lounging and socializing. You are going to need your own camping supplies such as a tent, ground rest, sleeping bag, cooking stove, pots and pans, etc.

Hostels: Contrary to popular belief, hostels are not dirty places to stay and are not full of hobos and derelicts. Hostels provide inexpensive basic accommodations to budget travellers. They offer varying sizes of dormitory rooms (same or mixed sexes) to private rooms. The majority provides common rooms to hang out and relax, and kitchens for cooking. This is probably the best mix of convenience and cost, and is the preferred place for backpackers to stay.

Hostels can be found nearly anywhere in the world. I have stayed in castles that had hostels inside of them to hostels that were actually permanently docked boats along the water front, or even small hostels hidden in the mountain range. Each had their own charm about them and offered a variety of amenities such as Internet, kitchens, common rooms, etc.

There are two distinct types of hostels: member or private. A member hostel is affiliated with an international hostelling group such as: Hostelling International (HI). HI is a huge network of over 4800 hostels in 60 countries offering clean and affordable places to stay for budget travellers. You will need to buy a membership at your local outdoor shop to get into these hostels (members only). Many of them can reserve (book-a-bed-ahead service) for free to other HI hostels on your route. They tend to uphold a higher standard and be slightly cleaner, but they are more sterile and institutional than private hostels. They enforce a lot of rules that must be followed. Some HIs have strict hours of operation like being closed between 10:00 a.m. and 4:00 p.m. It is advisable to inquire ahead of time.

Private hostels have all the amenities as member hostels, but tend to be more social and definitely have more character. Some have bars and discos in them, special event days, BBQs, outings, etc. They are usually more social and "hip" than member hostels and the price is nearly identical. My preference is staying in private hostels.

The seasons also play a big factor on the type of hostels I use. During the low season there are fewer tourists, prices tend to be lower, and hostels are not as booked. You can move about with a lot less stress about getting a room for the night. On the flip side, as the seasons start to warm up, more people are moving and travelling. This fills up the cheap hostels and sometimes you are forced to find other accommodations off the beaten path and usually pay more. I tend to go to HI hostels since you can easily have the staff phone and book a bed ahead. They deal with figuring out the phone system and foreign languages.

Guest houses: These are private houses whose owners rent out rooms to travellers. Depending where you are, they greatly vary in price and amenities. Most of the guest houses that I stayed in were located in South East Asia. Usually you get a single or double room and either a shared or private bathroom. It is a wise idea to ask if the room comes with hot water and insist on checking out the room ahead of time before committing to staying there.

Bed and Breakfasts (B&Bs): These are more expensive than hostels and cheaper than hotels. They offer you more of the homey type of atmosphere and a breakfast in the morning.

B&Bs are usually located outside of the business district and more into the residential areas or city limits.

Hotels: When everything else is booked up and you don't wish to sleep in the train station, you can always check into a hotel. I have stayed in many one-star hotels that offer you the basic bed, sink, and closet with a shared bathroom down the hall. The price is comparable to, if not a little bit more expensive, than a hostel. Even though you have the room totally to yourself and the key, keep all of your valuables locked up in your pack. The hotel cleaning staff still has access to your room. Of course, the higher the star of hotel, the better quality and higher the cost for the room.

Train and bus stations: In my travels I have been lucky enough to have a roof over my head every night. I have heard of other backpackers ending up sleeping in the open for the night and if you're lucky, you could get a couple hours of needed sleep. I do not recommend this, but when you are out of options this is one that you could choose. Use your common sense when sleeping in an open area and be careful.

My accommodation preference

There are places everywhere in the world where you can safely find a place to sleep for the night. Choosing a place that you find acceptable depends on personal preference, how much money you are willing to spend and how far out of your way are you willing to walk to get to your new 'home', the cleanliness of the place, how secure it is etc. The following is a list of things that I immediately look for when I step into a new "home for the week".

Close to transportation and downtown: Having a base close to the action and to the bus or train station is what I usually give preference to. Being close to the train/bus station means that you are not carrying your gear for kilometres navigating through a strange city. Plus you won't be trying to figure out obscure bus routes in a brand new city where you may not speak the language. Being downtown gives you convenient access to all the amenities and not a long walk back home at night.

A dorm room in a hostel: They are the cheapest and most social of all the places where you could stay. There are mixed or single sex dorm rooms and some have lockers where you can safely store your pack. The down side is that you are sharing it with other people who snore, make noise, turn on the room light, etc. when you are trying to sleep. This is where the earplugs and a sarong acting as a blindfold over your eyes comes in handy.

Self-catering kitchen: This will save you a lot of money on food and time looking for that cheap place to eat somewhere in your new city. Sometimes there is just a basic hot plate and basic utensils while others have full cooking stations complete with microwave, fridge, ovens, sink, and pots and pans and you are able to store your food in the fridge.

Common room: This is where you are going to find your new friends for the duration of your stay. This is the place where you find the backpacker community. Also, if you are tired and want a safe place to hang out, watch TV, read a book, and talk to someone, this is the place to do it. It is a great way to meet other travellers and provides a relaxing social setting.

Hot water: In a lot of the warmer climates, some of the guest houses don't have running hot water. If you are there during low season when the prices are lower and temperatures also lower, it is not pleasant trying to get yourself clean.

Security: If I have my own room, I always insist on taking my room key with me. I want to ensure that I always have access to my gear when I need it. During my travels, I have never been forced to return the room key when I step out. Sometimes they ask for it, but I just don't give it back. I don't want anyone to know when I am gone or have access to the room with everything I own in one bag.

I'm settled. What now?

Once you arrive at your new destination, you should find out what is currently going on. One of the best resources you have is the local tourist agency. You may have visited one when you first arrived looking for a place to stay. It is worth a second check since you now have time to spend exploring the area. These agencies are there to work for you. They offer free information on up coming attractions and keep various flyers and entertainment guides in stock.

> Note: Many cities have bus routes specifically for tourists. For a fee you can take these buses and discover more about the city. If you want to save some money, use the map and walk the route.

You may have an opportunity to hook up with some locals. Most of the time, they want to make sure you have a good time and want to show you the best of their country. They can also show you to the places where backpackers or tourists don't usually (or shouldn't) frequent. Since they live there they already know what places to avoid and where the hidden gems are located. If you are lucky, you can sometimes crash at their place and have use of their facilities.

And always use common sense. If you get a bad vibe from a person, just go and do your own thing.

Remember, it is up to you to have fun and find activities that interest you. Try to put in the effort to 'attempt' something new. Just remember this: "I may love it or I may hate it, but I will never know unless I try it".

Paying for stuff

If I am in a foreign country, what is the best way to pay for things? Hands down, the best way is paying in cash in the local currency. Then use your credit card as a backup. If you are desperate, go cash in some of your travellers' cheques.

Whenever you arrive in a new country with its own unique currency, look for a bank machine. Nearly every country and city in the world have these automated tellers. Make sure that you are on one of the networks displayed with – Cirrus™, Interac™, Electron™, etc. and your bank card should work just fine.

The amount you take out is up to you. I ask myself, how much money can I take out at one time that I can afford to loose and what is enough for me to take out to avoid using these machines again since the service fees are going to seriously add up? Sometimes you have to pay to take the money out of your account, a network fee, a trans-country fee, and the local banking fee. It adds up.

Sometimes it is a challenge to know how much you need to take out from a bank machine. Arriving in a new country, you find an ATM at a currency exchange agency and you are presented with the option of taking out 100, 10000, 100000, or 1000000 notes. Without knowing the value of the currency, you have no idea what is too much or what is too little.

Travellers' cheques should be avoided in my opinion. Each broker is different and can take as much as 20% for their cut and then you have to pay the current exchange rate. You just hope you bought them at a lower rate than you are exchanging them for. However, they are good even if you lose them. Make sure you record all of their serial numbers and denominations in your notes. If you misplace them or they get stolen, you can have them replaced.

Note: Make sure your wallet with some of your money is stored in a zipped pocket or inside your jacket or shirt. A wallet is easily stolen from your back pocket. Keep the rest safely in your money belt which is secured to your body. Your wallet may also carry some of your identification and is worth the extra effort to keep safe.

Your guidebook will give you generally how much your hostel and food will cost. They all come with a currency conversion chart and a big disclaimer that exchange rates change daily and it was accurate at the time of printing only.

If you travel to a place that has changed its currency or is not listed in your guidebook, you can still estimate how much things are going to cost before you arrive. Do some homework on what the current exchange rate is between your current country and your new one. I would expect the costs for services to be roughly the same between countries. For example, if accommodations cost 200 in my current country's currency, and the exchange rate is 1 to 2 ratio for the next country, I could approximate that I would be paying 400 in my next country's currency for my accommodations.

When you arrive, it's always good to do some detective work. Take a walk into a supermarket or a store and check out some of the prices. From there you can make a more educated guess on how much to take out.

When you are ready to make a purchase, be aware of how much of what you are buying is worth in your currency. Sometimes stores take advantage of backpackers who don't understand the currency and raise prices on us. And always count the change you are getting back. Often they will hand you back a pile of change and expect you to accept it. Count it! It is easy to short change someone who doesn't understand all the strange currency. In some countries, the smaller the coin, the more value it carries. Be careful.

Where to find food

Backpackers live on a budget and eating inexpensively is sometimes difficult. Travelling to a different country where the food is unrecognizable and the menu is equally incomprehensible makes life a little more challenging. It was in my sixth month of travelling when I stopped eating for taste. Eating became purely a nutritional activity to stay alive.

When first walking the streets of a new city in a foreign country, you have no idea of where the good places are. Sometimes you end up walking blocks and blocks, looking for a suitable place. When looking for a new place to eat, try to look for the busy restaurants that are populated by locals. If the locals eat there, it is more likely to be good food for the price. Eateries populated with tourists tend to be more of the tourist trap nature and are more expensive. Before eating at a place, ask for the menu and check the prices yourself.

As always, just be cautious of the quality of the food you are getting from any restaurant or vendor. You can always refuse the meal or send it back. Sampling the local food is a great idea; sampling the local bacteria is not.

The best places to eat are:

Local's homes: Sometime you meet a local and are invited for a meal. Not only can you get a free authentic home cooked meal for yourself, you get to share in their culture and tradition.

Supermarkets: Buy where the locals buy their food. Sometimes you are making your best guess on what you are buying since you can't read the local language. Most hostels have cooking facilities and cooking for yourself saves you a lot of money and gives you a social time with other backpackers.

The larger the supermarket usually means cheaper the food and larger the selection. It pays to shop around and do a price comparison. If you stop at the local corner store, you can expect to pay a little more for what you get. Another challenge is trying to decipher what you are actually buying. Sometimes the pictures don't represent what is in the carton.

University cafeteria: They cater to students who don't have t much money and poor cooking skills. This is a great place to go for an inexpensive hot meal. Most people think that the universities are strictly for students. But I have never been asked to produce a student card at the counter. They happily take my money and I walk out with the food.

Hostel store: Sometimes the hostel has a small shop dedicated to servicing those eating on a budget. The prices are competitive, if not a little more expensive.

Vendors on the street: The street vendors don't have all that extra expense of having a building where customers get the luxury of sitting down and being served. This gets us the food at a lower price. Try to pick a popular stall and, if you can, watch how they make your meal. It is probably the best way to do some quality control.

Fast food places: Check out the pizza, kebob, or falafel places over your traditional western fast food giant chains. These places are usual the staple diet for a lot of budget travellers. It is usually clean, fast, tasty, and semi-healthy for you.

Restaurants: You pay more for the service and atmosphere, but the food is usually better and selection greater. If you are going to choose a restaurant, the best way to gauge how good it is, take a look inside. If it if full of locals, it's probably a good spot to dine.

What I cook

Most hostels have a small compliment of pots and pans that you can use. What to buy to eat is always a challenge.

Here is a list of what I like to eat:

Pasta with sauce: quick, easy, cheap. Just add water and boil.
Frozen pizza: many types of toppings, just heat it up.
Cous cous with cup-a-soup: tasty. Just add water and boil together.
Musseli with yogurt: my usual breakfast. Even eat dry muesli from the box.
Frozen veggies: need your greens sometimes, just add water and heat up.
Bread with jam or cheese: fast and easy and doesn't require any utensils.
Instant rice with cup-a-soup: add hot water and mix.
Gazpacho: I hate the taste but it's good for you, as it is made from pure vegetables.
Microwave dinners: makes you look like the iron chief in minutes.
Cookies/biscuits/chocolate/trail mix: great for travelling and emergency food.
Instant mashed potatoes: surprisingly tasty and transportable.
Canned food: open it up and eat.
Fresh fruit with veggies: and it's even good for you.
Cereal in a box: just add milk or pour directly into mouth.
Multi-vitamins: just add water or any of the above.
My ultimate: instant mashed potatoes + cup-a-soup + pasta.

Note: Australians (Aussi) eat Vegemite and New Zealanders (Kiwis) eat Marmite. If you are not an Aussi or Kiwi and it is offered to you……just say "No!"

How to do laundry

When you run out of clean clothes to wear, it is time to do laundry. Sometimes half the day is gone just doing what little laundry you have since you have to do everything yourself in a new city. Just remember, by using the inside out method (wearing your underwear and socks inside out on the second day of use) works only once per article of clothing.

Here is the list of places where you can do laundry:

Friend's place: The best place to do laundry is at a friend's place. They may have laundry facilities on location and you would do best to take advantage of this. You don't have to worry about leaving your laundry drying out in the open where anyone could walk up to it.

Hand wash: All you need is to invest in a box of detergent and a clothes line. All hostels have sinks that can be used for washing your clothes. My first time doing this, it took me over three hours of washing, re-washing, and a third wash until the water turned a more or less clear color. After being satisfied that I got most of the dirt out of the clothes, I had to squeeze and wring out the water by hand. Depending on where you are, how ventilated the place is and how warm it is, it may take your laundry a day, to a day and a half to dry. There are times when I used the hand dryer at a local restroom to dry some clothes that I needed right away.

Laundromat: These are the second least expensive and a good way to get your clothes cleaned and dried in one place. After hand washing clothes for a month or so, take everything to the laundry mat to have them washed well. Many Laundromat's will provide you with soap and fabric softener for a small fee.

Hostel or hotel service: Be careful of using this service. It is fast, convenient and relatively safe, but you are going to pay for that extra service. There have been times where some articles are missing or delayed in getting back to you. Most times it is charged by weight. Make sure that you take the time to do the math to see how much it is going to cost you.

Dry cleaners: I avoid them. They provide you with the full service for a price. You give them your dirty clothes and within a couple hours they come back neatly folded and ironed in a bag, they even match up your socks. Convenient, but you are going to pay for that service.

Internet resources while travelling

The Internet is a great resource while travelling overseas. Every country that I have travelled to has Internet at varying reliability, speeds and price. Nearly every city I have been in has an Internet access point. Usually they are located all in the same area but the prices can vary from shop to shop. I like to do a little price comparison before I choose a place. Some places charge by the minute or every half hour, hour, etc. Just be careful and do the math to find the best deal.

The best place to use the Internet is where it is free. If there is a library or university near by it pays to walk inside and find the computer room. At the library you usually have to ask at the front counter. Even if you don't have a library card and you're not a resident of the country, you can, more often than not, get a computer for usually half an hour to an hour. At the university, find out where the computer lab is and just start using the Internet.

Here are some of the resources that may be useful to you when travelling:

Consulates: Sometimes you need to contact your Consulate, get a visa or other information on a foreign country. In many cases, your guidebook has the list of which Consulates are present in a particular city but the complete list is on the Internet.

Search Directory:
http://directory.google.com/Top/Society/Government/Embassies_and_Consulates/

Newsgroups: Ask a question, anything you want about backpacking, and someone will answer it for you. These are special newsgroups that are populated by newbie to veteran backpackers to share information and give recommendations. Many times when I couldn't find a particular answer, I posted the question to a newsgroup and it was answered by other backpackers who have "been there, done that." This is a great resource for anyone to use.

Internet Address + Search Directory:
http://thorntree.lonelyplanet.com

http://dir.groups.yahoo.com/dir/Recreation___Sports/Travel/Backpacking

Hostels: Many public and private hostels have websites where you can check location, bed availability, and prices. Some of them even allow you to reserve online.

Internet Search Directories:
http://directory.google.com/Top/Recreation/Travel/Lodging/Hostels/

http://dir.yahoo.com/Business_and_Economy/Shopping_and_Services/Travel_and_Transportation/Lodging/Hostels/

Maps: Internet maps are nice if you need to find a place. I don't spend a lot of time on this one myself, but I have seen other backpackers with printouts of the location of their next hostel on one of them.

Internet Search Directories:
http://directory.google.com/Top/Reference/Maps/

http://dir.yahoo.com/Science/Geography/Cartography/Maps/Interactive/

Currency converters: It is always nice to know how much your currency is worth compared to the current currency you are using.

Internet address:
http://www.xe.com/ucc/

Tour operators: If you want to put your feet up and let someone one else do the hard work for you and loose a little freedom, a tour operator could be the thing for you.

Internet search directories and addresses:
http://directory.google.com/Top/Recreation/Travel/Specialty_Travel/Backpacking/Tour_Operators/

http://dir.yahoo.com/Business_and_Economy/Shopping_and_Services/Travel_and_Transportation/Tour_Operators/Bus_Tours_and_Charters/Hop_On__Hop_Off_Buses/

Pay your bills: Many banks offer Internet banking to check your account balances, pay bills, transfer money, etc. I would be cautious of using this service in public Internet cafes because it is easy for a person to place a keystroke logger or another means of recording the current session and saving it all for review later.

Internet Search Keywords:
{your bank's name}

News: I like to be informed about what is happening in the world while I am travelling. If there is going to be another war happening, I want to know well before they start and steer clear of that country for a while. I try to find a non-government sponsored news website that can give me an unbiased view of the current country. Any government-sponsored news agencies tend to distort the news and be overly nationalistic in their reports. Try to find the local newspapers or local news on line to get the best and most detailed information.

Internet Search Directories:
http://directory.google.com/Top/News/

http://dir.yahoo.com/News_and_Media/By_Region/Countries/

Burning CDs: I have taken over 4000 pictures with my digital camera and the majority of Internet cafes were able to take my pictures from my camera and burn them to a recordable CD (CDR). Make sure that you bring all the cables, and software that came with the camera. To save some money, drop by a local computer store and buy one blank CDR there. The Internet cafes usually charge you a premium for blank CDR's.

When you burn a CD, do a single session burn instead of a multi-session burn. A single session burns copies all of your data to a CD and then finalizes the disc so that it can be read in other CD-ROMs. A multi-session burn allows you to keep burning information to the CD but it may not work in other CD-ROMS and if you don't use the same software to finish off the CD, you may destroy all the contents on the CD. When you finish burning a CD, put it in a safe place in your pack and forget about it. When the time comes to burn another CDR, buy a new CDR and use that one to store your pictures. This way, if you lose a CDR, or it gets damaged, you only loose 100 pictures instead of 1000s.

Be a diplomat

When travelling, you are actually a representative for your own country. Whomever you meet while travelling, you will be giving that new person a perspective on what people are like from your own country. Since they may have never been to your country, whatever impressions you give them reflects on your country. Some backpackers excel at being good ambassadors by showing mutual respect for differences, learning the art of listening, and generally being interested in the other country's culture. Unfortunately, others fail miserably and generally make themselves and their country look like arrogant idiots.

It is always a good idea to be on the locals' good side. You never know when you are going to need their help or advice. The following are some common sense suggestions on how to get along with local people and be a good ambassador for your country.

Leave your country at home: You travelled how far to experience something new? The last thing a local person wants to hear is how great your country is compared to how backward their homeland is! This is your chance to start learning and exploring other cultures. There are going to be 1001 things that are going to be different and easy to complain about. But this is the reason why you travelled in the first place: to get out of your comfort zone at home and experience what life is like someplace else. Be respectful. Remember that being different is not bad, just different from what you are used to. Learn to adapt.

Don't be loud and obnoxious: No one likes the loud mouth. When you enter a room, it is sometimes easy to tell who the foreigners are. They are talking loudly and shouting to one other, making huge gestures, and causing a regular disturbance. All the locals are doing their best to ignore them. Try to blend in. Before you start shouting or causing a scene that would be completely appropriate back at home, check out how everyone else is acting. It will be greatly appreciated by the locals and your fellow travellers.

Change the way you speak: When you are speaking to a local person, understand that English may not be their first, second, or even third language. They are doing their best to communicate with you, in their country, in your language. Don't take speaking your language for granted and expect them to understand. Make it easier for them. Start by slowing down your words, enunciate, stop using slang, and talk more with your hands. Some travelers make the mistake of speaking louder, believing that it would help get the point across. It really doesn't work. Don't start speaking louder, they are not hard of hearing and it's embarrassing to watch.

Try to speak their language: If you have a clue on how to speak their language, do it. It shows that you are trying to communicate, if not rather poorly, but it shows the effort. Often, a local will be more helpful and more forgiving if you switch to your own language.

Their English is not your English: There are subtle and potentially embarrassing situations where one culture would use a certain word and that word would have a completely different and sometimes vulgar meaning in the other culture. Just remember, you do not speak English, you speak a specific regional dialect of English. Let this be a chance to expand your vocabulary and enjoy the differences. My spoken English was vastly different than the Irish and Scottish English that I encountered.

Learn to listen: Don't push your values or ideas on the locals. Try showing some genuine interest in understanding their lifestyle and culture. Again, you are here to explore a new land, not to promote your own.

Do what the locals do: It will give you a chance to mix in and experience what life is like. This is all part of the adventure. This is why we travel. Go to where the locals eat and avoid the tried and true fast food eateries that you have back at home. You may even like it. The locals know the best spots since they live there.

Respect dress codes and local customs: The big thing is to blend in and work with the local people. Women especially will attract a lot of unwanted attention if they are not sensitive to local dress codes. In Arab countries for example, find out if it is socially acceptable before wearing tank tops, swim suit tops, or short skirts in pubic. Although it may be hot out, you don't need local men harassing you because they think you are easy. Adapt to and respect their local sensitivities. Remember that you are a guest in their country.

Adapt to their measurements: Learn both the Metric and Imperial system and use them correctly when speaking to someone. The majority of the world uses the metric system (kilometres, Celsius, etc) with the exception of the few who use the Imperial system (miles, Fahrenheit, etc) such as the U.K. and U.S.A. Also, learn the currency conversion rate from your country's money to theirs. Don't expect a local to know how much something costs in your own currency.

Change your body language: Gentle smiles are and likely to put both you and the person you are speaking with more at ease. Body language and facial expressions can vary greatly from country to country, but smiles are universal.

And always, learn to respect and accept the people for who they are. Try to break away from all the cultural stereotypes that your culture has programmed you to believe. Leave all of that at home. No culture is better or stronger, just different. Understanding this will help you find that travelling and relationships become a lot easier and more enjoyable.

Backpacking community

Many backpacker communities exist all throughout the world. The only membership needed into this group of world travellers is a backpack and a sense of wanderlust. Membership is free and it forms the basis of the backpacker social and support group.

So where do I find these transient communities? Just go where backpackers go. The best place is a hostel. It is easy to find someone or a group of people to hang out with. Everyone there automatically has something in common: they are away from home and are travelling just like you. Gone are most of the social pressures that you feel at home.

I have joined a group of backpackers at train stations just as everyone is disembarking or even while riding the bus. They stand out since they all carry large backpacks and are thumbing through a guidebook. It is nice to have someone with you when you arrive in a new city. Most of the time, they already know the ropes on how to travel and makes working together easier. Often they haven't booked their accommodations either and it's usually cheaper if you split the cost of a room.

Friends are easy to come by when you arrive at your new destination. Usually in the hostel you just walk up to a table, sit down, and start up a conversation. The conversation always seems to go something like this: Where are you from? Where have you gone? What is cool to do around this area? This is one of the best sources of accurate information and finding out what is worth seeing around the area.
From there it is easy to make plans and temporarily join up with another person or a group. You may even exchange e-mail addresses just before you part ways. Ironically, first names are usually the last things to be exchanged. It's just that the average backpacker relationship lasts for around four days before you part ways, it's hard to keep track of everyone's first names.

If you don't like or don't get along with the group that you are in, it is easy to find another group or travel solo. You shouldn't be worried about being "all alone in a strange country" since many other backpackers travelling are "all alone is a strange country" as well.

Travelling with a friend

This may sound like the only and safest way of travelling at the start. You have someone that you trust and can help you out if anything happens to you. Just be careful who you choose as your travelling companion. Travelling together has been known to be stressful and cause a lot of tension. You are suddenly forced to do everything together, all day and night without a break.

If you are going to travel with a friend, I would suggest that there be an understanding. You are not married to each other. You are there to hang out together and support each other. This means that if you want to do something and your friend doesn't, no problem, do the thing you want to do and meet up later. If you want to leave some place and your friend wants to stay, again no problem, you leave and your friend catches up to you later on. There is no written rule that you are going to have to compromise and agree upon everything that happens within the day. It is better to enjoy doing your own thing than grudgingly go with your travel buddy to do something that you don't find interesting.

Both of you can always stay in touch via e-mail and if one of you gets into trouble, you have someone to count on that is in the local vicinity. It's always great to catch up on, "What did you do?" stories when you hook up in the future.

It is also easy to find travelling companions while you are on the road. Backpackers commonly stay in the same type of accommodations and generally have a basic idea of where they are going. If you "click" nicely with someone, it's easy to hook up and travel with them. The same rules apply, you are not married or responsible for your new found travel buddy.

When you need help

While travelling, you will be in strange and new territory, and you will be placed into unfamiliar situations. Sometimes you may need to call upon someone for assistance in these cases. There are many people and resources you can call upon for aid.

Other backpackers: All backpackers will go out of their way to help you. Even if you don't know who they are, you are able to approach anyone for help. They are a wealth of information, and, in most cases, they have been through what you have and can give you suggestions and help.

Tourist agency: People who work in the tourist industry are an excellent source of help. They usually have information at hand on who to contact and can act as translators. They also provide free maps, lists of inexpensive hotels and hostels, up-coming events, and any other information that you may require to get around. This is the first place I look for when I first arrive in a new place.

Tourist police: These are special police trained to handle any kind of crime that happens to tourists. Many are open at all hours of the night and provide interpreters for you to communicate to the police. Their sole purpose is to keep the tourists and the tourist industry safe in their country.

Consulate: Your country's government has representatives abroad that can provide limited support in legal matters, visa or entry requirements, and general questions. It is important to remember that embassies deal with countries, and consulates deal with people. Sometimes they are combined into one but if you show up at your country's embassy, you will be asked to go to the consulate.

Locals: I have found that in most foreign counties, people are generally nice and willing to help out a stranger. There are many times when I approached someone on the street to ask for directions, or at least show them an address, and they would point me in the right direction.

Hostel or hotel staff: Even if you are not staying at that particular four-star hotel, the staff which are usually friendly to foreigners and are willing to assist you. Often, I would enter a posh hotel (tuck in my shirt and fix up the hair) and ask for a map or directions to a certain location and they would happily oblige.

Don't be afraid to ask for help. A lot of times I would find a convenience store or idle pedestrian on the street and ask them a quick question. There has never been a time when I was snubbed or looked down on. If you don't speak the same language, you can use your map and sign language to communicate.

Budget backpackers' tour groups

Instead of doing all the work of picking the next destination, searching for the next place to stay, and finding something fun and interesting things to do in your next city, you can enrol yourself in a backpacker tour group. These groups are designed to take backpackers to various locations on a budget.

You will be picked up by a "luxury coach" (a bus) at a predetermined location and time. On the bus will be other backpackers that have signed up for the same tour. This is a great way to make some quick new friends. You can hang out with them while you go out exploring. The tour operators will usually provide you with a guide that will try keep the group together, tell you about the local history of the area, and show you around to all the points of interest.

When you arrive at your next destination, the bus will drop you off right in front of a hostel. All you have to do is grab your gear from the storage compartment and check into your prebooked room. You have an option of joining the tour group or doing your own thing to explore your new destination.

Depending on where you are and the tour company you are with, you have a set amount of time per stop. In some cases, if you do want to stay longer, you can opt to take the next tour bus that the company has scheduled to arrive. This is called the "jump on, jump off" service. The tour package provides the transportation and rooms while you are free to do what you want when you are settled.

The tour company takes a lot of the unknown out of backpacking. There is a lot less stress and work involved by this way of travelling. No more arriving in a new place and trying to figure out where to stay for the night or figuring out where you are going to go next. It's all done for you.

This may sound like the safest and easiest way to travel throughout the world. To be honest, I have only tried this means of travel once and it lasted for a total of two weeks. You are stuck on a preset route that doesn't allow for much deviation. One of the things about backpacking that I enjoy is the freedom of choice. I can choose when I want to leave and how far I want to travel based on what is of interest to me. I also like to choose who I travel with. There are only a few times I came across the loud, arrogant, and generally, ignorant backpackers that I would rather not hang out with. When I take a day trip to visit someplace, I would rather have the opportunity to see it at my own pace instead of hearing, "You now have twenty minutes to walk around before the bus leaves." I also like checking out a few hostels before choosing one. Just comparing the condition of the rooms and the price before I commit to one is nice.

Where to go next

You decide that you have seen everything you want to see and it's time to find your next destination. Like most backpackers, you travel without a preconceived plan or itinerary. The big question is: where do I go next? The good news is that you are now in an environment where you have all the accurate and free information at your disposal. This information is more accurate and relevant than what you would have got at home when you first thought that making a detailed itinerary was actually a good idea.

At this stage of your backpacking tour, being shackled to an itinerary is unthinkable. It becomes a burden to follow a preconceived timetable that you made in another country.

Here you start to find out where all the interesting places in the world are. A lot of them cannot be found on the Internet or in a travel guide.

Before you start to choose where you want to go next, just remember that: you may love it or your may hate it, but you never know unless you go there. You will never have perfect information on you next destination.

When deciding, don't be overly picky about your next stop. Each place offers something unique and new. Every time we go someplace else, it's a small controlled leap into the unknown. This is all part of the adventure and fun of backpacking. I have been surprised and amazed at what a small insignificant village could have so much going for it. Based on everything I saw, it was a dot on a map and a convenient spot to spend the night. And always, if you decide you don't like where you are, just leave the next day.

Your guidebook will give you a general overview of what is offered. The information contained is from other backpackers and traveller writers who had previously visited the area and submitted write ups. They try to be as accurate as possible and cover most of the major features of the area that would interest you.

Your fellow backpackers at the hostel are an excellent source of information. They are travelling and staying in the same places you are and usually are checking out the same things that you are interested in. They can give accurate information on where to stay, where to eat, what to do, and things to avoid. This is by far your best source of advice.

The hostel staff are pretty knowledgeable as well. Catering to backpackers on a day to day basis and being from the local area they know the types of places we like to go to. Sometimes the hostels offer special travel packages customized for us at a decent price. It is sometimes worth checking into.

Tourist information is a good choice as well. They are mainly focused on dealing with requests within the local area or city. So if you are travelling some distance, their information could be limited. However, they can provide you with information on getting out of the city and the transportation schedules.

Locals are a good source of information but are sometimes a little bias. They want you to see the most and best of their country and would give you an entire run down on all the places you should visit. When I was in Spain for my first time, I started talking to a local and he started listing off every city in my guidebook explaining how I could not miss any one.

How and when I move

You have seen everything you want to see and are now ready to travel to your new destination. How do you do that safely and relatively inexpensively?

This is dependent on your current country. The general rule that I follow is to travel the way the locals do. Local people already know the best routes and modes of transportation.

If you have a couple of choices of what transportation to take, do your homework and compare some prices. Choosing to travel during non-peak times in a lower class coach on a week day could save you some money. Using a student card could also save you an additional 10 to 15% on the cost of the ticket.

Depending on the way you travel, and your finances, you could look into buying a pass. Many train and bus lines have a plethora of different passes that are available to the public. Make sure that it fits the way you travel. Some passes allow you unlimited travel within a certain number of days. If you find that you are spending up to a week or more in one destination, it may not be economical for you to have this kind of ticket. However, if you were travelling for only a short time and wanted to cover large distances this ticket may be worth the money.

The day that you travel is also important. I generally try to avoid travelling on Fridays and Saturdays for two reasons. First, these are the days when the hostels are most likely to be booked. I like to have a choice of hostels instead of trying to find the one in town that is empty. The worst case would be that you could be forced to find more expensive accommodations such as a hotel or you could end up sleeping in some bus or train station. Second, if any event is going to happen, it usually starts on a Friday or a Saturday. You could end up missing something interesting while riding on the bus, train, etc.

Sundays are best to avoid as well. When you are arriving in a new location, a lot of the time you are dependent upon city transportation and stores being open to find food, information, etc. On Sundays, many of these services are open for a limited time. Sundays are okay for finding accommodations since many people check-out on Sundays to get back to work for Monday. The optimal time to move cities are from Monday to Thursday. This way you get access to all services and know that the stores are open longer hours.

The type of transportation that you take is not important. The main goal here is to arrive at your destination safety and relatively inexpensively. Again, use what the local people use to travel. Here are just some of the modes of transportation I have taken:

- Buses (primary source of transportation, usually cheaper than trains).
- Trains (whenever a bus was not available).
- Rental car (amazing freedom to explore where tourists don't go).
- Minivan (Vietnam border crossing).
- Speed boat (over 6 hours on the Mek Kong river).
- Theonqew (converted pickup trucks in Thailand).
- Tuk Tuk (chainsaw engine powered three wheeled buggies in Thailand).
- Elephant (out back in the Asian jungle).
- Tram (to some mountain resorts in Malaysia).
- Subway/light rail transit (lots of cities have these).
- Ferry (going to various islands).
- Cruise ship (slept on the floor and partied all night).
- Airplane (sometimes the cheapest way to travel – budget carriers).

Internet Search Directories:
http://directory.google.com/Top/Recreation/Travel/Transportation/Air/Budget_Airfares/

When visas are important

To a backpacker, a visa is the country's governments way of collecting a tax off of foreigners who want to visit and a way of getting more money from them if they stay over their time limit. Officially, it is a means of governmental control to ensure they screen whoever enters into their country, limit what they can do, and limit the length of stay. Overall, it's just some extra work that you are going to have to do to enter into the country.

A visa is often a full page sticker that a country's consulate will place on a blank page within your passport. Its purpose is to give the border guards clear information on: when you are allowed to cross into their country, how long you are able to stay in the country, and place restrictions on your activities (being able to work, go to school, etc).

Finding out if you require a visa is part of your research when you decide to cross over into another country. If you have to get a Visa or specifying which types of visas you are eligible for is completely up to that country's local government. Go on the Internet and check with your country's Department of Foreign Affairs and International Trade (DFAIT) for that particular country's entrance requirements. Don't rely on your guidebook's stated entry requirements. Depending on how a specific country feels towards another will dictate what is required. They may change suddenly and without warning.

There are several different types of visas you can apply for. The following is a list of visas that are commonly used by backpackers.

Transit: This means that you are passing through the country and not planning on staying any particular period of time. This visa is usually valid for one or two nights. Most times they enforce that you must enter via one border crossing and leave via a different one. If the country has strict entry requirements, such as you have to have an invite in or a pre-booked accommodation and haven't done that, use this visa. It will get you a small taste of the country and let you into the next country on your route.

Tourist single entry: This is the most common visa that allows you to enter once through one border crossing, stay for a specific allotment of time, and leave via the same or different border crossing. You can leave through any border crossing to another country that you like, even the one you came in from. If you want to go back into the country, you will need to purchase another visa.

Tourist multiple entries: You are allowed to leave the country and then return without needing to reapply for a visa. These tend to be more expensive than single entry visas. If you know that your travels will take you back to this country, a tourist multiple entry visa is the more cost effective.

Student: You are allowed to attend school in that country, but not to work.

Work: You are allowed to seek employment in the country. These are usually hard to get, take a long time to be processed and cost a fair bit. Many times you have to be sponsored by a company that can prove that you have the skill sets to do the job and no one else in their country can. You have to apply for this visa while in your own country.

Residency: You are allowed to live in the country, go to school, and work. Being backpackers, we never get these visas.

Once you have determined that you need a visa, there are several steps you have to take before you can finally get that visa in your passport. On average it takes me one to three days before I receive a visa from a consulate.

Start by researching the entry requirements for the country. Check out the destination country's website since it is important to know the rules on how to get into to the country. In general, to apply for a visa you are required to produce two passport photos, your passport, a completed form, and money. For stricter countries, you may need to be 'invited in' by someone who is already a resident of that country, produce specific travel insurance or have your travel itinerary pre-booked in advance.

Once you have gathered the required items and information, you have to find your destination country consulate in your current country. The consulates are usually located in one of your current country's major cities. Your guidebook and the Internet are great resources to find the location and operating hours of a specific consulate. Make a note of the operating hours, some are open strange hours and can be a little frustrating if you finally find the place and it's closed.

When you finally arrive at the consulate, you will have to fill out a couple forms stating your personal information and intention for entering into the country. They will ask you to surrender or "give" your passport to them. Make sure you get a receipt. You will need to present the receipt to them to get your passport back. The process usually takes a couple of days. If you are in rush and need a passport faster, many of them offer rush services where they can have the visa done for you while you wait. This usually costs a premium.

If you want to be lazy and spend some extra money, you can let a hotel or travel agency do it for you. It does take a bit longer and you have to trust them with your passport. What they do is have you fill out all the necessary forms in the comfort of your hostel/hotel and then have someone go to the consulate and apply for your visas. Once the passports are ready to be collected, the agent will go to the consulate, pick up the passports and drive back and hopefully find you. You will have to pay the standard visa processing fee plus extra for the service. I would strongly recommend against this. Always do it yourself. Never be caught in a foreign country without your passport!

Border crossings

'It was the best of times, it was the worst of times'. A border crossing can be quick and easy or just a living hell depending on which country you are going through, your nationality and the particular mood of the border guard. I have had some pretty challenging border crossings in Asia and Eastern Europe, while others were easy

Before you cross a border and enter into a new country, I always like to pack some extra things to potentially make the trip more enjoyable. There have been times when the borders are closed or you are detained for some reason so bring the following:

Bottled water: around one to two litres of water.
Food: anything non-perishable that can give you energy if you have to miss a meal or two.
Money: the country's currency or American money. This is in case you arrive in the country and the banks are closed and you can not find an ATM machine.

You always have to cross two borders since you exit one country and enter another country. There is always a couple hundred meters of "no man's land" between the border controls.

The first border crossing is for you to get your exit stamp on your passport. It is basically the same if you are crossing via a train or the bus. Once you come close to the border you will be given an exit card to fill out. Here is where you fill out a bunch of personal information about yourself and write down anything that you have to declare.

Sometimes the border guards will come on board your transport and collect your passport and exit card. They take it back to the station where they process the batch and give them back to you once they are done. If they don't come onto the bus, everyone will be asked to come into the station and queue up individually to process your passports. At the end of the process you will receive an exit stamp next to your entry stamp for that country on your passport.

If you have overstayed your allotted time in the country, make sure you have enough money to pay the fine and provide a really good reason. Contact your embassy or consulate to see what exactly will happen to you.

The second border crossing is for your new entry stamp in your passport. This is sometimes a little harder than your exit stamp. You have to fill out an entry card and show them your passport. Sometimes all they will do is go through your bags or ask for secondary identification. To cross some other country's borders, they actually go as far as to take your photograph and fingerprints! Just remember, when you are crossing into another country you are going to have to play by their rules. In most cases you will be asked a series of questions. These officials are trained to filter out potential 'undesirables' from entering into the country. This is probably the most difficult part of the entire process. Depending on the mood of the border guard, you may have an easy time or a difficult time. When answering their questions, be as honest and to the point as possible.

Here is a list of questions that I was asked during one border crossing:

- What is your profession in your home country?
- How much money do you have on you?
- What are your limits on your credit cards?
- How much do you have in your bank account?
- How long are you going to stay?
- How long are you travelling for?
- What are you planning on doing while you are here?
- Where you are staying and what are you going to see?
- Do you have any friends here?
- Are you going to stay with them?
- Are you planning on marrying your friend?
- Which country did you come from?
- Which country did you start your travels from?

- How long did you stay there? Note – they asked me this question twice.
- What did you do in your previous country?
- Are you bringing anything from there with you into this country?

Buying souvenirs

Part of the fun of travelling is picking up curious items and gifts to show people back home, but there are a couple of things to keep in mind. Make sure that you have room in your backpack and are willing to carry all the odds and ends you pick up along the way. If you go on a spending spree, consider mailing your extra goodies home in a package rather than tote them around for the entire duration of your trip.

Be careful when buying skins, furs, animal-by-products and knives. It is hard to tell what is endangered and what is not. Each country has different rules for what they will and will not allow you to bring across the border. It is generally not worth the trouble, and in some cases, you can face a hefty fine or even put you in jail.

There may be ample opportunity to purchase pirated or imitation goods overseas. Doing this and sending them back home via the post is frowned upon by any local government. When you are sending items back home, you have to declare what the contents are. If you are suspected of sending illegal goods, it is a possibility that your package back home could be confiscated, be fined or serve a jail term.

Each country has different export laws. It is best to enquire at the local post office about what is allowed. In some cases, if you can not send something from one country, just wait until you are in your next country and send it from there.

Note: One time, my travelling buddy was going to send a cook book home. The employee at the post office said that they are going to have to charge him per page to read this cook book to make sure that he is not sending any "governmental secrets" home. He just put the cookbook back in backpack and sent it home when he arrived in our next country.

Staying healthy

If you don't have your health, you don't have anything. Staying in good health on the road is important and should not be neglected. The best advice is to exercise your common sense and listen to your body. You can do things to prevent getting sick.

Make sure you have the proper gear and equipment for the current climate and activities. If what you have is not keeping you warm and dry, strongly think about investing in something of better quality. Visit the local stores and do some shopping. Remember, your health and future enjoyment is riding on what you buy.

Take a look at your current lifestyle. Travelling is sometimes a lot of work. You are carrying your backpack sometimes for long periods in a new environment and climate. Over time, you may start to feel a little run down and tired. Take time to rest for a day or two. Walk to a local library and read some magazines or spend some money and visit the local leisure centre. Sit in the hot tub for a while or do a small workout.

Always try to eat and rest well. You may want to splurge and go to a restaurant or to an all you can eat buffet. Choose something healthy and filling on the menu. You may also want to supplement the meal with some of your multivitamins. Back at the hostel, you may want to splurge again and ask for a private room. There you can spend more time in bed without

the hassle of other packers snoring, making noise, or generally disturbing a much needed sleep.
Staying hydrated is important. Bottled water is the best thing drink. Drinking tap water is generally not safe and best avoided whenever possible. Sometimes you may see the locals drink tap water but realize that you do not have the local immunities that they do. Also, not all bottled water is the same. Try to buy bottled water with the natural minerals in it. Some bottled water is pure H_2O with all the minerals removed. Ensure that the seal is still on the bottle before you accept it.

You also have a support group. I have found that everyone is generally good and will try to do what they can to help you in your travels. Backpackers, hostel staff, and even the locals can help you find specific medical attention. If you have a specific type of allergy or have medication, feel free to tell your fellow backpackers and what they can do to help.

Keep in mind what the travel nurse warned you about when entering into this country. The local population has a natural immunity to a lot of the local ailments that you may not have. Try to be diligent in taking whatever medicine is prescribed in an infected area.

I want to highlight the importance of using your common sense and listening to your body while travelling. If you are feeling tired, get some rest. If you are hungry, get something to eat. Keeping yourself safe and healthy is the paramount concern while travelling.

Staying in touch

Keeping in contact with your friends, other backpackers, and family is essential. Not only does it provide you with a support line in case anything happens, it is a way of keeping relationships going and a feeling that you are not completely cut off from home. There are many ways of doing this.

Internet: Before you leave, set up an e-mail account or a blog site. This is by far the easiest way to stay in touch with everyone.

Instant messaging: Instant messaging on the Internet is a popular and inexpensive method of interacting with someone or a group of people around the world. Nearly all of the Internet cafes around the world have one type of instant messaging program installed. Save yourself some trouble and sign yourself up for an account before you leave home.

Phone: This is definitely more direct and personal than e-mail, but quite a bit more expensive and sometimes confusing to use. The cheapest way is to find a call box. This is a business with a bank of phones that offers long distance calls at a discount price. You walk into a booth and make all the calls you want, and when you are done, walk to the cashier and pay for all of your calls. You don't need a pocket full of change to use these phones. The cashiers will also show you how to correctly dial long distance in their country.

It is always good to co-ordinate ahead of time when you are going to reach someone. On average I was plus or minus 9 time zones away from my home at any given time. If you phone in the afternoon for a little chat, you may be waking someone up really early in the morning. The only time I used the phone was to call ahead for a few hostels and phone my family (very rarely). I always preferred e-mail.

If you are going to be using pay phones, it is a good idea to get a phone card. Many tobacconists and tourist centres sell phone cards. Each country has their own type of phone card and some may not work when you cross the border. If you do decide to get a phone card, make sure you are instructed on how to call long distance or overseas. Sometimes the phone cards help system is in that country's language. Without someone there to interpret, you could have purchased a useless phone card.

Post: Snail-mail is something that my parents did, and I have never bothered to use extensively. I guess it is nice to receive a hand written letter a couple weeks after it has been written with a picture on it, but I have always been more of the type to use a digital picture and send it via the e-mail (my bias).

I have seen many backpackers send mail such as postcards and souvenirs via the post office. Sometimes a shop owner will try to oversell you on stamps, capitalizing on the idea that you do not know and are unfamiliar with the currency. If you are at the post office, have them validate the stamps while you are there. Sometimes, they peal off the stamps when you are not looking and resell them to the next backpacker.

Working overseas

This is always a great idea, not only to supplement you dwindling finances, but also as a way to set down some temporary roots and get to know the local area better. However, many backpackers work "under the table" or illegally in other countries. If you are caught, it is a good way to get deported. Don't take the risk, you are there to travel and explore. You have all the opportunity in the world to work when you get back to your own country.

Unfortunately, I have never worked overseas. Everything in this guide is based on my experiences so this section is going to be a little brief. I have come across several backpackers who were working odd jobs at hostels and restaurants. There were work permits, visas, and bureaucracy red tape to go through for them to work there. Most of the jobs I was offered while travelling were under the table work but my focus was on traveling instead of working.

There are a lot of opportunities to work overseas. Here is a quick list to get you started:

Your Government: Many governments have already laid the ground work for their citizens to work overseas. These special work programs are usually for anyone between the age of 18 and 30. They provide the legal framework for you to find work in a number of countries while you provide everything else: transportation, day to day costs, finding a place to stay, etc.

Internet Keyword Search:
{your country} + work programs overseas

Private agencies: There are numerous private agencies that specialize in finding temporary job placements overseas. They work in conjunction with various governments to find and place prospective candidates.

Internet Search Directory:
http://directory.google.com/Top/Society/Organizations/Student/AIESEC/

http://dir.yahoo.com/Business_and_Economy/Employment_and_Work/Careers_and_Jobs/Jobs/Foreign_Employment/

Internet Keyword Search:
work abroad

Teaching English: This is probably the first thing someone thinks of when first considering about working overseas. We know the language and teaching something that we are already good at should be an easy way to make money. There are a lot of resources that are offered to assist you in this.

You can check into the TEFL (Teach English as a Foreign Language) or TESOL (Teachers of English to Speakers of Other Languages) program. These are two highly regarded Certifications to help placement agencies find you a job overseas.

Internet Search Directory:
http://directory.google.com/Top/Arts/Education/Language_Arts/English/English_as_a_Second_Language/Employment/

http://dir.yahoo.com/Business_and_Economy/Business_to_Business/Education/Employment/English_as_a_Second_Language/

Wwoofing: World Wide Opportunities on Organic Farms is the international organization to helping those who would like to volunteer on organic farms internationally. I have met a lot of travellers on the road who do this. They would apply to volunteer to work on a farm in exchange for free room and board. Some farms are great where they feed you a lot, the rooms are clean and spacious and have a lot of free time, and others are not so hot. You always have the option of leaving at any time.

Internet address:
http://www.wwoof.org/

Volunteering: This cuts into your traveling freedom but it is a great way to help people that are really in need. Also, it gives you a way to meet other like minded people and see how some of the local people live. Depending on which organization you choose to volunteer with and how long, some of your basic needs will be taken care of.

Internet Search Directory:
http://directory.google.com/Top/Recreation/Travel/Specialty_Travel/Volunteering/

http://dir.yahoo.com/Society_and_Culture/Issues_and_Causes/Philanthropy/
Community_Service_and_Volunteerism/International/

Internet Keyword Search:
volunteer abroad

Coming home

Introduction

You finally made it home. Your feet touch the same ground where you started your backpacking experience. You have done it. Congratulations! It really wasn't that hard after all. You now have more stories of adventure and travelling around the world to share with your friends and family. You are looking forward to some of the comforts of home. For you to, once again, hang out at some of your favourite spots and sleep in your own bed.

Now you have another challenge ahead of you. You have changed and so have your family and friends. This section is all about how to readjust back to your home culture. For some people, it is easy but, for others, it is quite difficult.

Reverse culture shock

You feel more versed, more experienced. You remember adjusting to the new culture, the new way of life and the jet lag that came from your long flight. The good news is that you have already experienced this and dealt with it, but now you are going to have to do it all over again.

You arrive home but it doesn't feel like home. You know that you have changed but so has your home. Walking once familiar streets feels different and foreign. Even your friends are different. It is like you do not even know them anymore. What is happening to you? You are experiencing reverse culture shock. This has been documented by many publications and affects people to varying degrees.

You have just experienced an amazing adventure full of challenges and stories. You just discovered how easy it was to move from city to city, and country to country. When you got bored of a place, you would just move to another. There you would make quick friends for a couple of days and start exploring and adventuring all the interesting spots. If you like your new place you would stay as long as you liked or if another opportunity presented itself you would jump on that next bus or train and start something new.

What to do now that you are back at home and not in some exotic location. Instead of a hostel, you have an apartment or your family's house. As for travelling to new cities on a whim, you are now stuck in one place for much longer than a week. Your friends have changed only slightly while you have grown so much in experience. No matter how good you are at telling your adventure stories, your friends just cannot relate to what you have experienced. You find that day to day, everything happens at a much slower pace than what you are used to. It seems that you have been travelling at 100 kilometres per hour, only to wake up the next day and find yourself down to a slow trot. Welcome to the reality of reverse culture shock or the backpacker's hangover!

Dealing with reverse culture shock

Here are some suggestions that have helped with reverse culture shock:

- Stay in touch with all of your friends that you made overseas. You have their e-mail address and pictures you can share with them.
- Look through all of your pictures you have taken and read through your journal. It's amazing what you have forgotten and what kind of memories come back.
- Do something new that interests you and avoid going back to your old habits. Basically, try not to fall back into your previous routine. You have an opportunity to start over again.

- Visit the backpackers' newsgroups on the Internet and give advice. Many times there are other backpackers in need information and post questions to the newsgroups. Share your experience/advice with others.
- Rebuild your new life with what you have learned while travelling. You are the new and improved version and can start fresh. Take advantage of this.
- Think about having daily adventures on more micro instead of a macro level.
- Walk through a new park, join a club, or take some interesting classes.

The travel bug

Even with the best medication in the world, there is no cure for the travel bug. We all acquire it while we are travelling the world. The symptoms start to surface a couple of weeks after we arrive home. It starts as a feeling that we want to go exploring again. Everything is boring at home. Nothing changes. It is like you have hit a brick wall. And you know something that no one else knows. Something you discovered while travelling. It is easy. For us, taking off to another country is like driving to a nearby city.

When you arrive back home, the first two weeks are all new and exciting. You are living high and revisiting all the places that you left behind. It's just like visiting a new place in another country. Checking out new and exciting places and meeting excellent and interesting people. But soon after all of that is done, what do you do now? The urge to get out of your current environment and back to travelling is pretty strong.

If I were offered a trip to anywhere in the world right now, I could be ready in under an hour if I was really interested in going. It is simply that easy now.

Readjusting

After the honeymoon of coming home has worn off, you are going to start noticing some differences around you. You don't feel like you are at home when you are at home. The once familiar streets and life seem to have changed. Even your friends seem different. Just like you, they have changed as well.

Readjusting is important to get back to your 'new' life style. You may have a big challenge ahead of you. There are lots of old established patterns or ruts that you can fall back into. You are now a different person with new experiences and perceptions. This is an opportunity to start again, and not fall back to what you were, but to keep growing. Do not try to fall back into your old lifestyle of who you were before you went travelling. Keep up the effort and make something new in an environment you already know.

Every day, you were adapting to new stimuli and challenges, why not keep using that skill to adapt back to your home? It does not have to feel the same as it did before you left. Take a walk down the street and see everything again for the first time, but this time, you don't need a guidebook or a back pack. Take in everything; just like when you were backpacking. If something is interesting, explore it. There is no fear or apprehension. Compared to what you experienced overseas, this is easy. This time your new activity can be something more long term since you will be staying here for a while.

Conclusion

So who am I now? What has all this time and expense of traveling the wold given me? Was it worth it? Where do I go from here?

My experiences have changed me. Fundamentally, I am still the same person, but I have a new outlook on life. I received some valuable advice when I was nearing the end of my travels from a fellow backpacker: "Don't forget what you have learned." He wasn't referring to the new languages I picked up, or the historical knowledge I accumulated or even the friendships I dearly would hate to give up, it was the life style. It was the fundamental backpacker life style that can be applied when you get home.

Each day, when I wake up in a strange and new country, I explore the unknown. I go out and look for new activities and new sources of knowledge. Be it a tour of an ancient ruin, a hike in a new mountain range, or scuba diving along a tropical island. There is an ongoing and constant way of living - change. I do not know what is out there. Exploring what is out there, living and adapting to new environments and best of all, knowing that I did it.

When you arrive back at home, do not fall back into your old, established life style. Basically, the same rut that you carved out for yourself before you left. Do what you did while you were traveling – try something new. You did it while you were traveling, why not do it when you get back home. It should be a lot easier, don't you think? You know the culture, the language, the people, etc. What is stopping you from choosing to live somewhere new, to try a new activity, or to do something you always were thinking about doing? Just remember that you have already done all of this – in a foreign country! Why is your home so different?

For me personally, when I walk outside, I no longer feel any apprehension about the unknown. I embrace it, I look forward to change. I almost crave it. No more mundane, repetitive lifestyle. After what I experienced, and the challenges I had to over come while travelling, everything here is pretty easy. Living here I have the comfort of a life where I speak the same language as everyone else. I have my own apartment, and a pretty good job that pays the bills. This is pretty easy living and yet we take it all for granted and become complacent.

I hope that you take the opportunity to travel and explore your world. There is so much out there that you don't know about. Don't fall into the mind set that I have heard from other people: "I live in the greatest country in the world, and have everything that I need. Why would I want to go any place else?" How would you even begin to believe that when you have never been to another country? Take off the blinders and get out of your country. You may be pleasantly surprised.

Life is way too short to spend laying on the couch watching TV or being excited when a new movie is going to be released to DVD. Although, that level of complacency is easy to fall into, it's predictable and comfortable.

There is so much more out there waiting to be discovered. Like the phrase: "The more you learn the less you know." It may sound grand that I have travelled the world through 30 individual countries. But after you do travel to 30 countries you realize that it is actually not a great accomplishment. It is just the first peak of a very big mountain. There is still much more climbing to do.

As with everything in life: you don't know if you are going to love it or hate it until you do it. Go on, take a chance, you just may discover a new way of living.

Acknowledgments

I would deeply like to thank everyone who have volunteered their talents in helping make this book a success.

Photo: Darcy Delainey

Sarah Eaton is the president and founder of Eaton International Consulting (EIC) Inc. (http://www.eatonintl.com/) and a personal friend of mine. Sarah speaks and teaches Spanish, and has dabbled in various other languages. She is an accomplished public speaker, author, and a fellow world traveller. It was her daunting task to be my editor and correct my numerous grammatical errors.

Kay Smandych assisted with the editing of this book. She has also traveled the world, generously donating her time and efforts to helping those in third world countries with social intervention and refugee work. The passion she has for other cultures and her compassion for people in need has influenced her in all she does, both professionally and personally. Her greatest legacy is her three sons who have also travelled extensively.

Ryan Mesenchuk designed the front and back covers. He wishes he had met Carl before deciding to travel through Australia with a full 70 litre backpack!

Andrea Newman loves shoes, lizards and dance. She designed my webpage for two Bellini's. To see more of her work visit: http://www.andreanewman.com/

I also would like to thank my parents and all the amazing people who I have crossed paths with during my travels? Each and every one of you has made this book possible

About the Author

Carl Fransen was born and raised in a small rural city of Nelson, nested in the mountains of British Columbia, Canada. He left his home town to pursue a career as a computer tech. Settling down in Calgary with a steady job, he started pursuing other interests.

Within a couple years, he became a competitive Latin dancer winning several competitions. With a strong interest in the martial arts and several years of training, he became a Hapkido instructor at Cutting Edge Hapkido. Wanting to improve his public speaking skills, he joined Toastmasters, taking on executive roles in his local club.

Not long afterwards, he caught the travel bug. Donning a backpack, Carl travelled across three continents on a quest of exploration, learning, and adventure. After 15 months, and 30+ countries later, he returned home to Canada. Inspired by his experience, he wrote *BACKPACKER: How to Travel the World*, and *BACKPACKER: The Journey Begins.*

He currently resides in Calgary, Canada as the owner of a successful IT business: CTECH Consulting Group.

Other Publications by Carl T. Fransen

visit:

http://www.aworldtraveller.com